Professional Resumes Series

RESUMES
FOR
SALES &
MARKETING
CAREERS

The Editors of
VGM Career Horizons

 **VGM Career Horizons**
a division of *NTC Publishing Group*
Lincolnwood, Illinois USA

Library of Congress Cataloging-in-Publication Data

Resumes for sales and marketing careers/the editors of VGM.

    p. cm.— (VGM's professional resumes series)
  ISBN 0–8442-8545-5 (softbound): $9.95
  1. Résumés (Employment) 2. Sales personnel. 3. Marketing.
I. VGM Career Horizons (Firm) II. Series.
HF5383.R45 1990   90–43351
650.14'024381–dc20   CIP

1992 Printing

Published by VGM Career Horizons, a division of NTC Publishing Group.
©1991 by NTC Publishing Group, 4255 West Touhy Avenue,
Lincolnwood (Chicago), Illinois 60646-1975 U.S.A.

  1 2 3 4 5 6 7 8 9 VP 9 8 7 6 5 4 3 2

ACKNOWLEDGMENT

The editors gratefully acknowledge Jeffrey S. Johnson for his help in the writing and production of this book.

CONTENTS

INTRODUCTION

Your resume is your first impression on a prospective employer. Though you may be articulate, intelligent, and charming in person, a poor resume may prevent you from ever having the opportunity to demonstrate your interpersonal skills, because a poor resume may prevent you from ever being called for an interview. While few people have ever been hired solely on the basis of their resume, a well-written, well-organized resume can do much more towards helping you to land an interview than a poor one can. Your resume's main purpose is to get you that interview. The rest is up to you and the employer. If you both feel that you are right for the job and the job is right for you, chances are you will be hired.

A resume must catch the reader's attention yet still be easy to read and to the point. Resume styles have changed over the years for the better. Today, brief and focused resumes are preferred. No longer do employers have the patience, or the time, to review two or three pages of solid type. A resume should be only one page long, if possible, and never more than two pages. Time is a precious commodity in today's business world and the resume that is concise and straightforward will usually be the one that gets noticed.

Let's not make the mistake, though, of assuming that writing a brief resume means that you should take less care in preparing your resume. A successful resume takes time and thought, and if you are willing to make the effort, the rewards are well worth it. Think of your resume as a sales tool with the product being you. You want to sell yourself to a prospective employer. This book is designed to help you prepare a resume that will help you further your career—to land that next job, or first job, or to return to the work force after years of absence. So, read on. Make the effort and reap the rewards that a strong resume can bring to your career. Let's get to it!

Chapter One

THE ELEMENTS OF A GOOD RESUME

A winning resume is made of the elements that employers are most interested in seeing when reviewing a job applicant. These basic elements are the ingredients of a successful resume and are essential to any resume. These elements become the actual sections of your resume. The following is a list of elements that may be used in a resume. Some are essential, some are optional, and we will be discussing these in this chapter in order to give you a better understanding of each element's role in the makeup of your resume:

1. Heading
2. Objective
3. Work Experience
4. Education
5. Licenses and Certificates
6. Professional Memberships
7. Honors
8. Activities
9. Special Skills
10. References

The first step in preparing your resume is to gather together all the information about yourself and your past accomplishments. Later you will refine this information, rewrite it in the most effective language, and organize it into the most attractive layout. First, let's take a look at each of these important elements individually.

Heading

The heading may seem to be a simple enough element in your resume, but take care not to take it lightly. The heading should be placed at the top of your resume and should include your name, home address, and telephone numbers. If you can take calls at your current place of business, include your business number, since most employers will attempt to contact you during the business day. If this is not possible, and you can afford it, purchase an answering machine that allows you to retrieve your messages while you are away from home. This way you can make sure you don't miss important phone calls. *Always* include your phone number on your resume. It is crucial that when prospective employers need to have immediate contact with you, they can.

Objective

When seeking a particular career path, it is important to list a job objective on your resume. This statement helps an employer to know the direction that you see yourself heading, so that he or she can determine whether your goals are in line with the position available. The objective is normally one sentence long and describes your employment goals clearly and concisely.

Below are a few examples of job objectives as they might appear on a resume:

Example #1
OBJECTIVE: To join a small- to medium-sized public accounting firm with a near-term goal of partnership admission.

Example #2
OBJECTIVE: To secure a position as a paralegal where I can utilize my education, my writing, and my interpersonal skills.

Example #3
OBJECTIVE: A professional sales position, leading to management in the food industry, where my administrative experience, communications skills, and initiative can be utilized to increase sales and improve customer relations.

As you can see, the job objective will vary depending on the type of person you are and the type of goals you have. It can be either specific or general, but it should always be to the point.

This element in some cases is not necessary, but usually it is a good idea to include your objective. It gives your possible future boss an idea of where you are coming from and where you want to go.

Work Experience

This element is arguably the most important of them all. It will provide the central focus of your resume, so it is necessary that this section be as thorough as possible. Only by examining your work experience in depth can you get to the heart of your accomplishments and present them in a way that demonstrates the strength of your qualifications. Of course, someone just out of school will have less work experience than someone who has been working for a number of years, but the amount of information isn't the most important thing—rather, how it is presented and how it highlights you as a person and as a worker will be what counts.

As you work on this section of your resume, be aware of the need for accuracy. You'll want to include all necessary information about each of your jobs, including job title, dates, employer, city, state, responsibilities, special projects, and accomplishments. Be sure to only list company accomplishments for which you were directly responsible. If you haven't participated in any special projects, that's all right—this area may not be relevant to certain jobs.

A basic rule of resume writing, and an extremely important one is: *List all work experience in reverse chronological order.* In other words, always start with your most recent job and work your way backwards. This way your prospective employer sees your current (and usually most important) job before seeing your less important past jobs. Your most recent position should also be the one that includes the most information as compared to your previous positions. If you are just out of school, show your summer employment and part-time work, though your education will most likely be more important than your work experience in this case.

The following worksheets will help you to gather information about your past jobs. Begin with your most recent job and work backwards.

WORK EXPERIENCE
Job One:

Job Title _____

Dates _____

Employer _____

City, State _____

Major Duties _____

_____

_____

_____

_____

_____

_____

Special Projects _____

_____

_____

_____

Accomplishments _____

_____

_____

_____

_____

_____

_____

_____

_____

Job Two:

Job Title _____

Dates _____

Employer _____

City, State _____

Major Duties _____

_____

_____

_____

_____

_____

_____

_____

Special Projects _____

_____

_____

_____

Accomplishments _____

_____

_____

_____

_____

_____

_____

_____

Job Three:

Job Title _____

Dates _____

Employer _____

City, State _____

Major Duties _____

_____

_____

_____

_____

_____

_____

_____

Special Projects _____

_____

_____

_____

Accomplishments _____

_____

_____

_____

_____

_____

_____

_____

_____

Job Four:

Job Title _____

Dates _____

Employer _____

City, State _____

Major Duties _____

_____

_____

_____

_____

_____

_____

Special Projects _____

_____

_____

_____

Accomplishments _____

_____

_____

_____

_____

_____

_____

_____

_____

Education

Education is the second most important element of a resume. Your educational background is often a deciding factor in an employer's decision to hire you. Be sure to stress your accomplishments in school with the same finesse that you stressed your accomplishments at work. If you are looking for your first job, your education will be your greatest asset, since your work experience will most likely be minimal. In this case, the education section becomes the most important. You will want to be sure to include any degrees or certificates you received, your major area of concentration, any honors, and any relevant activities. Again, be sure to list your most recent schooling first.

The following worksheets will help you to gather information for this section of your resume. Also included are supplemental worksheets for honors and for activities. Sometimes honors and activities are listed in a section separate from education, most often near the end of the resume.

EDUCATION

School _____

Major or Area of Concentration _____

Degree _____

Date _____

School _____

Major or Area of Concentration _____

Degree _____

Date _____

School _____

Major or Area of Concentration _____

Degree _____

Date _____

Honors

Here, you should list any awards, honors, or memberships in honorary societies that you have received. Usually, these are of an academic nature, but they can also be for special achievement in sports, clubs, or other school activities. Always be sure to include the name of the organization honoring you and the date(s) received, e.g. Dean's List, 1989, 1990. Use the worksheet below to help gather your honors information.

HONORS

Honor: _____

Awarding Organization: _____

Date(s): _____

Honor: _____

Awarding Organization: _____

Date(s): _____

Honor: _____

Awarding Organization: _____

Date(s): _____

Honor: _____

Awarding Organization: _____

Date(s): _____

Activities

You may have been active in different organizations or clubs during your years at school, and often an employer will look at such involvement as evidence of initiative and dedication. Your ability to take an active role, and even a leadership role, in a group should be included on your resume. Use the worksheet provided to list your activities and accomplishments in this area.

ACTIVITIES

Organization/Activity: _____

Accomplishments: _____

_____

_____

Organization/Activity: _____

Accomplishments: _____

_____

_____

Organization/Activity: _____

Accomplishments: _____

_____

_____

Organization/Activity: _____

Accomplishments: _____

_____

_____

As your work experience increases through the years, your school activities and honors will play less of a role in your resume, and eventually you will most likely only list your degree and any major honors you received. This is due to the fact that, as time goes by, your job performance becomes the most important element in your resume. So, through time your resume should change to reflect this.

Certificates and Licenses

The next potential element of your resume is certificates and licenses. You should list these if the job you are seeking requires them and you, of course, have acquired them. If you have applied for a license, but have not yet received it, use the phrase "application pending."

License requirements vary by state. If you have moved or are planning to move to another state, be sure to check with the appropriate board or licensing agency in the state in which you are applying for work to be sure that you are aware of all the necessary requirements.

Always be sure that all of the information you list is completely accurate. Locate copies of your licenses and certificates and check the exact date and name of the accrediting agency, e.g., Teaching Certificate, State of Illinois Board of Education, 1988. Use the following worksheet to list your licenses and certificates.

CERTIFICATES AND LICENSES

Name of License: _____

Licensing Agency: _____

Date Issued: _____

Name of License: _____

Licensing Agency: _____

Date Issued: _____

Name of License: _____

Licensing Agency: _____

Date Issued: _____

Professional Memberships

Another potential element in your resume is a section that lists professional memberships. Use this section to list any involvement in professional associations, unions, and similar organizations. It is to your advantage to list any professional memberships that pertain to the job you are seeking. Be sure to include the dates of your involvement and whether you took part in any special activities or held any offices within the organization, e.g., United Garment Workers Association, Secretary/Treasurer, 1984–1989. Use the following worksheet to gather your information.

PROFESSIONAL MEMBERSHIPS

Name of Organization: _____

Offices Held: _____

Activities: _____

Date(s): _____

Name of Organization: _____

Offices Held: _____

Activities: _____

Date(s): _____

Name of Organization: _____

Offices Held: _____

Activities: _____

Date(s): _____

Name of Organization: _____

Offices Held: _____

Activities: _____

Date(s): _____

Special Skills

This section of your resume is set aside for mentioning any special abilities you have that could relate to the job you are seeking. Today, many employers seek applicants that have experience with computers. Be sure to list all types of computer hardware and software with which you have familiarity. Often, knowledge of a particular type of software is essential if the particular company you are interviewing with uses it exclusively. This is the part of your resume where you have the opportunity to demonstrate certain talents and experiences that are not necessarily a part of your educational or work experience.

Another beneficial special skill is knowledge of a foreign language. Just open a newspaper to the classified section, and you will notice the numerous job openings for those with bilingual skills. Be sure to mention if you are fluent or simply have a working knowledge of a foreign language. This will make a difference to your employer.

Special skills can encompass a wide range of your talents—from being a freelance editor to being an expert pilot. Remember to be sure that whatever skills you list relate directly or indirectly to the type of work you are looking for.

References

References are not usually listed on the resume, but a prospective employer needs to know that you have references who may be contacted if necessary. All that is necessary to include in your resume regarding references is a sentence at the bottom stating, "References are available upon request." This will suffice. A prospective employer may indeed wish to have a list of references, so be sure to have your list ready before you send out your resume. Also, check with whomever you list to see if it is all right for you to use them as a reference. Forewarn them that they may receive a call regarding a reference for you. This way they can be prepared to give you the best reference possible.

Chapter Two

WRITING YOUR RESUME

*N*ow that you have gathered together all of the information for each of the sections of your resume, it's time to write out each section in a way that will get the attention of whomever is reviewing your resume. The type of language you use in your resume has a profound effect on its success. You want to take the information you have gathered and translate it into a language that will cause a potential employer to sit up and take notice.

Resume writing is not like expository writing or creative writing. It embodies a functional, direct writing style and focuses on the use of action words. By using action words in your writing, you more effectively stress past accomplishments. Action words help demonstrate your initiative and highlight your talents. Always use verbs that show strength and reflect the qualities of a "doer." For example, instead of "Put together a sales plan for the Midwest," use "Orchestrated a regional sales plan that increased sales in several midwestern states." Instead of "The newspaper was redesigned while I was managing editor," say "Served as managing editor. Redesigned newspaper's layout." By using action words, you characterize yourself as a person who takes action, and this will impress potential employers.

One sure way to identify a verb is the fact that it can usually take an *-ed* ending to form the past tense. Another way to identify a verb is to try to use the word *I* in front of it. The following is a list of verbs commonly used in resume writing. Use this list to choose the action words that can help your resume become a strong one:

administered	introduced
advised	invented
analyzed	maintained
arranged	managed
assembled	met with
assumed responsibility	motivated
billed	negotiated
built	operated
carried out	orchestrated
channeled	ordered
collected	organized
communicated	oversaw
compiled	performed
completed	planned
conducted	prepared
contacted	presented
contracted	produced
coordinated	programmed
counseled	published
created	purchased
cut	recommended
designed	recorded
determined	reduced
developed	referred
directed	represented
dispatched	researched
distributed	reviewed
documented	saved
edited	screened
established	served as
expanded	served on
functioned as	sold
gathered	suggested
handled	supervised
hired	taught
implemented	tested
improved	trained
inspected	typed
interviewed	wrote

Now let's take a look at the information you put down on the work experience worksheets. Take that information and rewrite it in paragraph form, using verbs to highlight your actions and accomplishments. "Here's an example:

WORK EXPERIENCE

Job Title: Regional Sales Manager

Dates: 1984–1988

Employer: Pillsbury & Co.

City, State: Levitown, PA

Major Duties: Manager of sales representatives from seven states. Responsible for twelve food chain accounts in the East. In charge of directing the sales force in planned selling toward specific goals. Supervisor and trainer of new sales representatives. Consulting for customers in the areas of inventory management and quality control.

Special Projects: Coordinator and sponsor of annual food industry sales seminar.

Accomplishments: Monthly regional volume went up 25 percent during my tenure while, at the same time, a proper sales/cost ratio was maintained. Customer/company relations improved significantly.

Below is the rewritten version of this information, using action words. Notice how much stronger it sounds.

WORK EXPERIENCE

Pillsbury & Co., Levitown, PA

Regional Sales Manager, 1984–1988

Managed sales representatives from seven states. Handled twelve food chain accounts in the eastern United States. Directed the sales force in planned selling towards specific goals. Supervised and trained new sales representatives. Consulted for customers in the areas of inventory management and quality control. Coordinated and sponsored the annual Food Industry Seminar. Increased monthly regional volume 25 percent and helped to improve customer/company relations during my tenure.

This is the kind of direct, strong language necessary for a successful resume. Another way of constructing the work experience section is by using actual job descriptions. Job descriptions are rarely written using the proper resume language, but they do include all the information necessary to create this section of your resume. Take the description of one of the jobs you are including on your resume (if you have access to it), and turn it into an action-oriented paragraph. Below is an example of a job description followed by a version of the same description written using action words.

PUBLIC ADMINISTRATOR I

Responsibilities: Coordinate and direct public services to meet the needs of the nation, state, or community. Analyze problems; work with special committees and public agencies; recommend solutions to governing bodies.

Aptitudes and Skills: Ability to relate to and communicate with people; solve complex problems through analysis; plan, organize, and implement policies and programs. Knowledge of political systems; financial management; personnel administration; program evaluation; organizational theory.

WORK EXPERIENCE
State of California, Los Angeles, California

Public Administrator I, 1985–1990

Wrote pamphlets and conducted discussion groups to inform citizens of legislative processes and consumer issues. Organized and supervised crew of interviewers. Trained interviewers in effective communication skills.

Now that you have learned how to word your resume, you are ready for the next step in your quest for a winning resume: assembly and layout.

Chapter Three

ASSEMBLY AND LAYOUT

*A*t this point, you've gathered all the necessary information for your resume, and you've rewritten this information using the language necessary to impress potential employers. Your next step is to assemble these elements into a logical order and then to lay them out on the page neatly and attractively so as to achieve the desired effect: getting that interview.

Assembly

The order of the elements in a resume makes a difference in its overall effect. Obviously, you would not want to put your name and address in the middle of the resume, or your special skills section at the top. You want to put the elements in an order that stresses your most important achievements, not the less pertinent information. For example, if you recently graduated and have no full time work experience, you will want to list your education before you list any part time jobs you may have held during school. On the other hand, if you have been gainfully employed for several years and currently hold a significant position in your company, you will want to list your work experience ahead of your education, which has become less pertinent with time.

There are some elements that are always included in your resume and some that are optional. On page 20 is a list of essential and optional elements:

Essential	Optional
Name	Job Objective
Address	Honors
Phone Number	Special Skills
Work Experience	Professional Memberships
Education	Activities
References Phrase	Certificates and Licenses

Your choice of optional sections depends on your own background and employment needs. Always use information that will put you and your abilities in a favorable light. If your honors are impressive, then be sure to include them in your resume. If your activities in school demonstrate particular talents necessary for the job you are seeking, then allow space for a section on activities. Each resume is unique as each person is unique.

Types of Resumes

So far, our discussion about resumes has involved the most common type of resume—the *chronological resume*. In a chronological resume, all work experience is listed in reverse chronological order with your most recent job first and so on. This is the type of resume usually preferred by human resources directors, and it is the one most frequently used. However, in some cases this style of presentation is not the most effective way to highlight one's skills and accomplishments.

For someone reentering the work force after many years or someone looking to change career fields, the *functional resume* may work best. This type of resume focuses more on achievement and less on the sequence of your work history. In the functional resume, your experience is presented by what you have accomplished and the skills you have developed in your past work.

A functional resume can be assembled from the same information you collected for your chronological resume. The main difference lies in the use you make of this information. Essentially, the work experience section becomes two sections, with your job duties and accomplishments comprising one section and your employer's name, city, state, your position, and the dates employed making up another section. The first section is placed near the top of the resume, just below the job objective section, and can be called *Accomplishments* or *Achievements*. The second section, containing the bare essentials of your employment history, should come after the accomplishments section and can be titled *Work Experience* or *Employment History*. The other sections of your resume remain the same. The work experience section is the only one affected in the functional resume. By placing the section that focuses on your achievements first, you thereby draw attention to these achievements. This puts less emphasis on who you worked for and more emphasis on what you did and what you are capable of doing.

For someone changing careers, emphasis on skills and achievements is essential. The identities of previous employers, which may be unrelated to one's new job field, need to be downplayed. The functional resume accomplishes this task. For someone reentering the work force after many years, a functional resume is the obvious choice. If you lack full-time work experience, you will need to draw attention away from this fact and instead focus on your skills and abilities gained possibly through volunteer activities or part-time work. Education may also play a more important role in this resume.

Which type of resume is right for you will depend on your own personal circumstances. It may be helpful to create a chronological *and* a functional resume and then compare the two to find out which is more suitable. The sample resumes found in this book include both chronological and functional resumes. Use these resumes as guides to help you decide on the content and appearance of your own resume. One example each of chronological and functional resumes follows on the next two pages.

Layout

Once you have decided which elements to include in your resume and you have arranged them in an order that makes sense and emphasizes your achievements and abilities, then it is time to work on the physical layout of your resume.

There is no single appropriate layout that applies to every resume, but there are a few basic rules to follow in putting your resume on paper:

1. Leave a comfortable margin on the sides, top, and bottom of the page (usually 1 to 1½ inches).

2. Use appropriate spacing between the sections (usually 2 to 3 line spaces are adequate).

3. Be consistent in the *type* of headings you use for the different sections of your resume. For example, if you capitalize the heading EMPLOYMENT HISTORY, don't use initial capitals and underlining for a heading of equal importance, such as Education.

4. Always try to fit your resume onto one page. If you are having trouble fitting all your information onto one page, perhaps you are trying to say too much. Try to edit out any repetitive or unnecessary information, or possibly shorten descriptions of earlier jobs. Maybe

CHRONOLOGICAL RESUME

GINA STEVENSON
433 Maple Drive
Hoffman Estates, IL   60035
708/555-2341

OBJECTIVE

To become a part of the sales and marketing team at Laura Ashley, Inc.

WORK EXPERIENCE

Gina Designs, Hoffman Estates, IL
Owner/Designer, 1980 - present
Established a national market for my original clothing line. Displayed
and merchandised clothing items at retail stores and fashion shows.
Increased sales 300% in the past two years. Ordered supplies, processed
purchase orders and invoices. Shipped and delivered products.

Talbot's Inc., Schaumburg, IL
Assistant Sales Manager, 1981 - present
Sold clothing and gifts at the retail level. Increased sales by developing
in-store sales promotions. Ordered stock and maintained inventory.

Lynn's Hallmark, Arlington Heights, IL
Sales Person, 1970 - 1974
Manager, 1975-1980
Managed gift shop and supervised 10 employees. Maintained inventory, sales
records and bank deposits. Ordered products, processed purchase orders and
invoices. Handled all payroll duties. Sold gift items.

EDUCATION

B.A., Interior Design, Wheaton College, Wheaton, IL, 1980

SPECIAL SKILLS

Working knowledge of Spanish.
Experience working with WORD PERFECT V & DISPLAYWRITE IV.

REFERENCES

Provided on request

FUNCTIONAL RESUME

Catherine Kaye
4301 Forest Park
St. Louis, MO 63212
314-555-8243 (w)
314-555-3538 (h)

OBJECTIVE: Political campaign or party managment

SUMMARY OF QUALIFICATIONS
— 15 years managerial and supervisory work in public service
— Project design and administration
— Staff recruitment, training and supervision
— Public and media relations
— Sophisticated research skills
— Community liaison
— Fund raising, grantmanship and fiscal management for budgets of several million dollars
— Expertise in political process and political action
— Campaign management for local union and school associations
— Excellent communication skills, both verbal and written
— Member/officer community action organization and local school associations

EMPLOYMENT HISTORY:

1980–PRESENT:	Managing Librarian Metropolitan Public Library, Florissant, MO
1975–1980	Supervising Librarian, Hollywood Branch, Los Angeles County Public Library
1968–1975	Social Sciences Librarian, Westwood Branch, Los Angeles County Public Library
1965–1968	Political Science Fellow, American Federation of State, County and Municipal Employees
1964–1965	Librarian Intern, City of Los Angeles Municipal Library

EDUCATION

MA—	University of Southern California—1968 Political Science/Public Administration
MSLS—	University of California, Los Angeles—1965 Certified Public Librarian
BS—	Pepperdine University—Malibu—1963 Sociology/Political Science

SPECIAL SKILLS
— DOS experience
— LOTUS/DBASE/WORDPERFECT

OTHER INTERESTS
— International Politics and Government
— Reading
— Travel

REFERENCES MAY BE OBTAINED UPON REQUEST

you've included too many optional sections. Don't let the idea of having to tell every detail about your life get in the way of producing a resume that is simple and straightforward. The more compact your resume, the easier it will be to read and the better impression it will make for you.

Try experimenting with various layouts until you find one that looks good to you. It may be a good idea to show your final layout to people who can tell you what they think is right or wrong with it. Ask them what impresses them most about your resume. Make sure that is what you want most to emphasize. If it isn't, you may want to consider making changes in your layout until the necessary information is emphasized. Use the sample resumes in chapter 5 to get some ideas for laying out your resume.

Putting Your Resume in Print

Your resume should be typed or printed on good quality $8^1/_2'' \times 11''$ bond paper. You want to make as good an impression as possible with your resume; therefore, quality paper is a necessity. If you have access to a word processor with a good printer, make use of it. If not, a typewriter that produces good, clean copy should be just fine.

After you have produced a clean original, you will want to go ahead and make duplicate copies of it. Usually a copy shop is your best bet for producing copies without smudges or streaks. Make sure you have the copy shop use quality bond paper for all copies of your resume. Ask for a sample copy before they run your entire order. After copies are made, check each copy for cleanliness and clarity.

Another more costly option is to have your resume typeset and printed by a printer. This will provide the most attractive resume, but most likely the neat, clean, hand-typed resume will have the same effect as the typeset resume at far less expense.

Proofreading

After you have finished typing the master copy of your resume and before you go to have it copied or printed, you must thoroughly check it for typing and spelling errors. Have several people read it over just in case you may have missed an error. Misspelled words and typing mistakes will not make a good impression on a prospective employer. They are a bad reflection on your writing ability and your attention to detail. With thorough and conscientious proofreading, these mistakes can be avoided. The following are some rules of capitalization and punctuation that may come in handy when proofreading your resume:

Rules of Capitalization

- Capitalize proper nouns, such as names of schools, colleges and universities, names of companies, and brand names of products.
- Capitalize major words in the names and titles of books, tests, and articles that appear in the body of your resume.
- Capitalize words in major section headings of your resume.
- Do not capitalize words just because they seem important.
- When in doubt, consult a manual of style such as *Words Into Type* (Appleton-Century-Crofts); or *The Chicago Manual of Style*, (The University of Chicago Press). Your local library can help you locate these and others.

Rules of Punctuation

- Use a comma to separate words in a series.
- Use a semicolon to separate series of words that already include commas within the series.
- Use a semicolon to separate independent clauses that are not joined by a conjunction.
- Use a period to end a sentence.
- Use a colon to show that the examples or details that follow expand or amplify the preceding phrase.
- Avoid the use of dashes.
- Avoid the use of brackets.
- If you use any punctuation in an unusual way in your resume, be consistent in its use.
- Whenever you are uncertain, consult a style manual.

Chapter Four

THE COVER LETTER

*O*nce your resume has been assembled, laid out, and printed to your satisfaction, the next and final step before distribution is to write your cover letter. Though there may be instances where you deliver your resume in person, most often you will be sending it through the mail. Resumes sent through the mail always need an accompanying letter that briefly introduces you and your resume. The purpose of the cover letter is to get a potential employer to read your resume, just as the purpose of your resume is to get that same potential employer to call you for an interview.

Like your resume, your cover letter should be clean, neat, and direct. A cover letter usually includes the following information:

1. Your name and address (unless it already appears on your personal letterhead).

2. The date.

3. The name and address of the person and company to whom you are sending your resume.

4. The salutation ("Dear Mr." or "Dear Ms." followed by the person's last name, or "To Whom It May Concern" if you are answering a blind ad).

5. An opening paragraph explaining why you are writing (in response to an ad, the result of a previous meeting, at the suggestion of someone you both know) and indicating that you are interested in whatever job is being offered.

6. One or two more paragraphs that tell why you want to work for the company and what qualifications and experience you can bring to that company.

7. A final paragraph that closes the letter and requests that you be contacted for an interview.

8. The closing ("Sincerely," or "Yours Truly," followed by your signature with your name typed under it).

Your cover letter, including all of the information above, should be no more than one page in length. The language used should be polite, businesslike, and to the point. Do not attempt to tell your life story in the cover letter. A long and cluttered letter will only serve to put off the reader. Remember, you only need to mention a few of your accomplishments and skills in the cover letter. The rest of your information is in your resume. Each and every achievement does not need to be mentioned twice. If your cover letter is a success, your resume will be read and all pertinent information reviewed by your prospective employer.

Producing The Cover Letter

Cover letters should always be typed individually, since they are always written to particular individuals and companies. Never use a form letter for your cover letter. Cover letters cannot be copied or reproduced like resumes. Each one should be as personal as possible. Of course, once you have written and rewritten your first cover letter to the point where you are satisfied with it, you certainly can use similar wording in subsequent letters.

After you have typed your cover letter on quality bond paper, be sure to proofread it as thoroughly as you did your resume. Again, spelling errors are a sure sign of carelessness, and you don't want that to be a part of your first impression on a prospective employer. Make sure to handle the letter and resume carefully to avoid any smudges, and then mail both your cover letter and resume in an appropriate sized envelope. Be sure to keep an accurate record of all the resumes you send out and the results of each mailing.

Numerous sample cover letters appear at the end of the book. Use them as models for your own cover letter or to get an idea of how cover letters are put together. Remember, every one is unique and depends on the particular circumstances of the individual writing it.

Now your job is complete. You can let your cover letter and resume do the rest and land you that interview that very well could lead to the job you are seeking.

Chapter Five

SAMPLE RESUMES

This chapter contains dozens of sample resumes for people pursuing a wide variety of jobs and careers in sales and marketing. There are many different styles of resumes in terms of graphic layout and presentation of information. These samples also represent people with varying amounts of education and work experience. Use these samples to model your own resume after. Choose one resume, or borrow elements from several different resumes to help you construct your own.

DONALD E. THOMPSON
1314 W. Dundee Road
Buffalo Grove, IL 60006
708/555-3909

JOB OBJECTIVE: Computer sales.

WORK
EXPERIENCE: Microtech Computers, Northbrook, IL
                      Account Executive, 1979 - present
                      Handled sales accounts for northwest suburban area.
                      Expanded customer base by 25% during my tenure.
                      Conducted field visits to solve customer problems.
                      Maintained daily contact with customers by telephone
                      to insure good customer/company relations. Wrote
                      product information fliers and distributed them through
                      a direct mail program.

                      IBM, Chicago, IL
                      Technical Support Specialist, 1971 - 1979
                      Installed and maintained operating system. Defined
                      and oversaw network lists and tables. Coordinated
                      problem resolution with phone companies. Performance
                      tuned subsystems and networks. Planned and installed new
                      hardware and programming techniques.

                      IBM, Chicago, IL
                      Systems Analyst, 1960 - 1971
                      Documented procedures for mechanization of payroll
                      department. Created standards and procedures for main
                      accounting system. Coordinated requirements meeting with
                      production department on new inventory system. Developed
                      test procedures for reverification of new application.
                      Developed distribution lists, user IDs and standards for
                      electronic mail system.

EDUCATION: Northwestern University, Evanston, IL
                      M.S. in Mathematics, 1959
                      Graduated with honors.

                      B.A. in Chemistry, 1956
                      Dean's List
                      Seabrook Scholarship

PROFESSIONAL
AFFILIATIONS: Computer Sales Association
                      Illinois Business Chapter

SEMINARS: Microtech Sales Seminars
                      IBM Technical Workshops

                      References available upon request

HANNAH GOLDSTEIN

1800 W. Pico
Santa Monica, CA 90110
213/555-8938
213/555-8000

JOB OBJECTIVE

A marketing/promotion position in the entertainment industry where I can ultilize my communication skills, contacts and industry background.

WORK EXPERIENCE

TBC MARKETING, Burbank, CA
Independent Marketing, 1988 - present
Coordinated stock with regional distributors. Generated exposure and interest at local retail store and one-stops in conjuction with local and regional airplay. Suggested supplemental marketing strategies based on airplay, sales and percentage of penetration.

HITS MAGAZINE, Van Nuys, CA
National Marketing Coordinator, 1986 - 1988
Sold charts and tracking information to radio, artist management and record labels. Handled tracking for all accounts on charting product. Interacted with radio accounts weekly regarding early chart information.

CASHBOX MAGAZINE, Los Angeles, CA
Regional Sales Representative, 1983 - 1986
Managed and developed west coast territory for Cashbox Service Network. Provided chart information, including bullet criteria, points, sales/airplay ratios to independent marketing companies and management. Serviced retail accounts and created new marketing strategies for product tracking services.

PARKER MANUFACTURING, Flint, MI
Sales Representative, 1979 - 1983
Negotiated and sold contract repairs on industrial equipment. Wrote daily technical reports on product movement and inventory. Consistently met and exceeded sales quotas for each quarter.

EDUCATION

MICHIGAN STATE UNIVERSITY, Grand Rapids, MI
B.A., Communications, 1979

REFERENCES

Available on request

HENRY JAZZINSKI
3000 Big Mile Road
Dallas, TX 84038
214/555-8888 (Daytime)
214/555-3839 (Evening)

OBJECTIVE

A management position in the sales and marketing field.

ACHIEVEMENTS

Sales

Increased watch sales from $3 million to $12 million during the past six years.
Introduced new and existing product lines through presentations to marketing directors of major manufacturers.
Developed fifteen new accounts.
Supervised five sales agencies throughout the U.S. and Canada.

Marketing

Developed new products expanding from watches to other accessories which resulted in increased sales.
Researched the watch market in order to coordinate product line with current fashion trends.
Increased company's share of the market through improved quality products.

WORK HISTORY

Culture Shock Watch Co., Dallas, TX
Vice President of Sales and Marketing, 1979 - present

Nabisco Food Co., San Francisco, CA
Sales & Product Manager, 1974 - 1979

Avis, Inc., Los Angeles, CA
Sales Representative, 1969 - 1974

EDUCATION

University of Southern California, Los Angeles, CA
B.S. in Business Administration, 1968

SEMINARS

Dallas Sales & Marketing Seminar, 1987 - 1990
National Marketing Association, 1982 - 1986

References available on request

SANDRA SORENSON

3201 W. Oerono St.
Apartment 23
Pittsburgh, PA 28901
412/555-9302
412/555-4209

JOB SOUGHT: Public relations director for the marketing division of a major candy manufacturer.

RELEVANT
EXPERIENCE: <u>Public Relations</u>

-Represented company to clients and retailers in order to present new products.
-Organized and planned covention displays and strategy.
-Designed and executed direct mail campaign that identified marketplace needs and new options for products.

<u>Management</u>

-Managed a sales/marketing staff which included account managers and sales representatives.
-Monitored and studied the effectiveness of a national distribution network.
-Oversaw all aspects of sales/marketing budget.

<u>Development</u>

-Conceived ads, posters and point-of-purchase materials for products.
-Initiated and published a monthly newsletter that was distributed to current and potential customers.

EMPLOYMENT
HISTORY: <u>Redboy Peanut Crunch</u>, Pittsburgh, PA
National Sales Manager, 1987 - present
Account Manager, 1985 - 1987
Assistant Account Manager, 1984 - 1985
Personnel Assistant, 1982 - 1984
Receptionist, 1980 - 1982

EDUCATION: B.A. in English, 1979
University of Pennsylvania, Harrisburg, PA

SEMINARS: American Marketing Association Seminars, 1985 - 1990

SPECIAL
SKILLS: Computer literacy in BASIC and FORTRAN. Knowledge of WORD PERFECT 5 and DBASE-III.

REFERENCES: Available on request

JANIS DARIEN

345 W. 3rd St.   Telephone: 617/555-3291
#42
Boston, MA 02210

JOB OBJECTIVE: To obtain a position as a marketing management trainee.

EDUCATION: Boston University, Boston, MA

                   B.A. degree in Economics, 1990
                   Dean's List four quarters
                   3.45 GPA in major field
                   3.21 GPA overall
                   Homecoming Planning Committe

                   Plan to pursue graduate studies towards a Master's degree
                   in Marketing at Boston University, Evening Division.

                   Central High School, Evansville, IN

                   Graduated 1986
                   Top 10% of class
                   Business manager and coordinator of student newspaper
                   Vice President of Senior class
                   Student Council
                   Pep Club

WORK EXPERIENCE: Lewis Advertising Agency, Boston, MA
                   Marketing Assistant, Summer 1989
                   Assisted Marketing Manager in areas of promotion, product
                   development and demographic analysis.

                   Paterno Marketing, Boston, MA
                   Telephone Interviewer, Summer 1987 & 1988

                   White Hen Pantry, Evansville, IN
                   Cashier, Summer 1986

SPECIAL SKILLS: Fluent in French. Familiar with various computer hardware and
                   software.

REFERENCES: Available on request

MELANIE B. MALONEY
1200 PUERTA DEL SOL
CHATSWORTH, CA 92203

TELEPHONE: 714/555-6789

OBJECTIVE: A job as a salesperson in a fine jewelry store.

RELEVANT
SKILLS: *Sold jewelry at a fine jewelry store.
                 *Greeted customers and advised them on their needs.
                 *Answered complaints from "problem" customers.
                 *Generated repeat business by encouraging customers to return.
                 *Designed jewelry displays for store.
                 *Entered data on computer to keep track of inventory.
                 *Handled returns and orders from distributor.

WORK
EXPERIENCE: Stacey's Jewelers, Chatsworth, CA
                 Sales Associate, 1988 - present

                 Eddy Gems, Glendale, CA
                 Sales Clerk, 1985 - 1987

                 Jones Day Care, Tempe, AZ
                 Art Teacher, 1985 - 1986

                 Parker Hardware, Robeson, AZ
                 Cashier, 1984 - 1986

EDUCATION: Tempe College, Tempe, AZ
                 B.A. in Art, 1985

HONORS: Tempe Honor Society, 1985
                 Velma G. Lydeckker Art Award, 1984

SPECIAL
SKILLS: Fluent in Spanish. Hands-on computer experience using d-BASE III.

REFERENCES: Available upon request

ELVIRA WASHINGTON

453 Franklin Ave.
San Diego, CA 94890
619/555-3489

OBJECTIVE

A management position in marketing where I can utilize my
promotion and public relations experience.

WORK EXPERIENCE

JUST PASTA INC., San Diego, CA
Marketing Director, 1986 - present
Developed a successful marketing campaign for a restaurant chain.
Initiated and maintained a positive working relationship with
radio and print media. Implemented marketing strategies to
increase sales at less profitable outlets. Designed a training
program for store managers and staff.

GREAT IDEAS CARPET CLEANING CO., Dallas, TX
Marketing Representative, 1982 -1986
Demonstrated carpet cleaners in specialty and department stores.
Reported customer reactions to manufacturers. Designed fliers
and advertising to promote products. Made frequent calls to
retail outlets.

REBO CHIPS, INC., Chicago, IL
Assistant to Sales Manager, 1977 - 1982
Handled both internal and external areas of sales and marketing,
including samples, advertising and pricing. Served as company
sales representative and sold potato chips to retail outlets.

EDUCATION

UNIVERSITY OF ILLINOIS AT CHICAGO, Chicago, IL
B.A. Marketing, 1976

SEMINARS

San Diego State Marketing Workshop, 1988, 1989
Sales and Marketing Association Seminars, 1984

References available on request.

MARY ALICE MOORE
3230 W. Alsip Drive #3C
Milwaukee, WI 53100
419/555-8908

OBJECTIVE: Marketing representative for a major U.S. airline company.

EXPERIENCE: <u>Midwest Airlines, Inc.</u>, Milwaukee, WI
Sales representative, 1988 - present
Sold reservations for domestic flights, hotels and car rentals. Marketed travel packages through travel agencies. Negotiated airline and hotel discounts for customers. Devised itineraries and solved customers' travel related problems.

<u>Travel in the Main</u>, Evanston, IL
Travel Agent, 1980 - 1988
Handled customer reservations for airlines, hotels, and car rentals. Advised customers on competitive travel packages and prices. Interacted with all major airlines, hotel chains and car rental companies.

EDUCATION: <u>University of Wisconsin</u>, Beloit, WI
B.A. in Anthropology, 1956

SPECIAL
SKILLS: Hands-on experience using most travel-related computer systems, including Apollo.

Working knowledge of German, French and Polish.

REFERENCES: Available on request.

JEREMY S. PANDY

1441 S. Goebert
Providence, RI   00231
401/555-1234
401/555-3782

Objective

President of a U.S. publishing corporation where I can apply my management, promotion and sales experience.

Employment History

JOHNSON PUBLISHING CORPORATION, Providence, RI
VICE PRESIDENT, 1980 - 1990

Promoted from Sales Manager to Vice President of Advertising after three years. Managed all phases of publishing properties including:

> Furniture Magazine
> Home Improvement Weekly
> Scuba Digest
> Travel Age Magazine
> Pharmacy News

Established and developed the first newspaper advertising mat service in the furniture industry. Increased distributors and retailers using this service by 55% in three years. Improved the effectiveness and volume of all retail advertising.

REBUS PUBLISHING COMPANY, Boston, MA
ADVERTISING MANAGER, 1971 - 1979

Serviced and developed accounts throughout the eastern United States. Handled advertising for publications in the restaurant industry. Increased sales in my territories every year by at least 21%.

TIME MAGAZINE, New York, NY
ASSISTANT ADVERTISING PROMOTIONS MANAGER, 1967 - 1971

Spearheaded original promotion program that increased revenue 33% in two years. Developed new markets. Helped to improve company/customer relations.

ROYAL CROWN COLA CORPORATION, Chicago, IL
DIVSION SALES MANAGER, 1964 - 1967

Promoted from salesman to sales manager after one year. Organized sampling campaigns and in-store and restaurant displays. Directed bottlers' cooperative advertising and point-of-purchase displays.

JEREMY S. PANDY - 2

Education

DRAKE UNIVERSITY, Des Moines, IA
B.A. in Economics, 1963
Graduated Phi Beta Kappa
Top 5% of class

Professional Affiliations

Rocking Chair, social and professional organization of the Furniture Industry
President, 1988 - 1990

Beverage Association of America
Board of Directors

Publishers Association
Advisory Committee

References

Available upon request

MICHELLE CRUMLEY
2316 SHERMAN AVE. #3B
EVANSTON, IL 60201
708/555-4727

EDUCATION: Northwestern University, Evanston, IL
Bachelor of Arts in Economics
Expected June 1991
GPA: 3.45

HONORS: Phi Beta Kappa
Dean's List Seven Quarters
Owen L. Coon Award, Honorable Mention

ACTIVITIES: President, Activities & Organizations Board
Wa-Mu Show
Captain, Soccer Team
Freshman Advisor

WORK
EXPERIENCE: Shand Morahan Insurance Co., Evanston, IL
Marketing Intern, 1990
Assistant Marketing staff in the areas of research,
demographics, sales forecasts, identifying new customers
and promotion.

Northwestern University, Evanston, IL
General Office, Registrar, 1988 - 1990
Processed transcript requests. Entered registrations
on the computer. Provided informational assistance to
students.

SPECIAL SKILLS: Knowledge of French & Russian. Experience using
WORDSTAR software.

REFERENCES: Available on request

DIANA FAGEN THOMPSON
8000 East Fifth Avenue
Silver Springs, MD 04890
202/555-8398

OBJECTIVE: A management position in sales or marketing.

EMPLOYMENT
HISTORY: **Interco.**, Washington, DC
              Regional Sales Manager, 1983 - present
              Managed sales of all product lines in eastern
              markets for a leading manufacturer of cotton
              products. Represented five corporate divisions of
              the company with sales in excess of $2 million
              annually. Directed and motivated a sales force of
              12 in planned selling to achieve company goals.

              Robertson Co., Miami, FL
              District Manager, 1978 - 1983
              Acted as sales representative for the Miami
              metropolitan area. Built both wholesale and
              dealer distribution substantially during my
              tenure. Developed monthly sales plans which
              identified necessary account maintenance and
              specific problems that required attention.

              Western Office Products, Inc., Sarasota, FL
              Assistant Sales Manager, 1969 - 1978
              Handled both internal and external areas of sales
              and marketing, including samples, advertising and
              pricing. Served as company sales representative
              and sold a variety of office supplies to retail
              stores.

EDUCATION: **Miami University**, Miami, FL
              B.A. in English, 1967

SEMINARS: American Sales Association Seminars, 1985 - 1990

REFERENCES: Available on request.

DAVID TERRENCE JOHNSON
5656 W. Ogden Ave.
La Grange, IL 60189
708/555-1828
708/555-2020

OBJECTIVE: Senior vice president of sales and marketing Ranco
Computers, Inc.

PROFESSIONAL
ACHIEVEMENTS: Sales

* Introduced new and existing product lines
through presentations to major clients.
* Increased sales from $27 million to $50 million
  in five years.
* Initiated and developed nine new accounts.
* Supervised five sales agencies throughout the
  U.S.

Marketing

* Researched computer market in order to
coordinate product line with current public tastes
and buying trends.
* Developed new approaches to marketing software
  products, including in-store displays and
advertising.
* Organized and planned convention displays and
  strategies.

EMPLOYMENT
HISTORY: Ranco Computer Co., Chicago, IL
Sales and Marketing Manager, 1985 - present

Unico, Melrose Park, IL
Product Coordinator, 1980 - 1985

Torvis Electrical Supply, Canoga Falls, NY
Sales Representative, 1975 - 1980

EDUCATION: New York University, New York, NY
B.S. 1975
Major: Business Administration
Minor: Computer Science

REFERENCES: Available upon request

TYRELL JACOBS, III

4504 Bloomfeld Ave.
Westchester, NY   12090
718/555-3849

JOB OBJECTIVE: A position as vice president of sales at
                        Clear Plastics, Inc.

PROFESSIONAL
EXPERIENCE: Clear Plastics, Inc., Brooklyn, NY
                        Sales Manager, 1985 - present
                        Sold custom designed point-of-purchase
                        elements and product displays. Researched
                        target areas and developed new account leads.
                        Researched and determined advertising in
                        national publications. Made sales
                        presentations to potential customers.
                        Participated in plastics industry trade
                        shows.

                        Westchester Tractor Co., Westchester, NY
                        District Sales Manager, 1981 - 1985
                        Planned successful sales strategies in order
                        to identify and develop new accounts.
                        Supervised seven sales representatives.
                        Increased sales by at least 20% in each of my
                        four years. Researched and analyzed market
                        conditions to seek out new customers. Wrote
                        monthly sales reports.

                        Brooklyn Freight Co., Brooklyn, NY
                        Account Executive, 1978 - 1981
                        Managed accounts in the New York metropolitan
                        area. Expanded customer base 30% in four
                        years. Maintained daily contact with
                        customers by telephone in order to insure
                        good customer/company relations. Wrote
                        product information fliers and distributed
                        them through a direct mail program.

EDUCATION: Harvard University, Boston, MA
                        M.B.A. with honors, 1977

                        Drake University, Des Moines, IA
                        B.A. in Accounting, 1974

PROFESSIONAL
MEMBERSHIPS: Brooklyn Sales Association, 1986 - present
                        New York Merchants Group, 1981 - present

REFERENCES: Available upon request

VONDA MAPLES

7777 W. Devon Ave.   312/555-8908
Chicago, IL 60646   312/555-7200

OBJECTIVE: Sales manager.

WORK
EXPERIENCE: Pier One Imports, Chicago, IL
                  Sales Coordinator, 1987 - present
                  Managed ten field representatives. Handled
                  information dissemination and distribution. Co-
                  designed a full-color catalog. Placed advertising
                  in major trade publications. Promoted products at
                  trade shows. Maintained inventory status reports
                  and personnel records.

                  Auburn Publishing Co., Lincolnwood, IL
                  Distribution Assistant, 1980 - 1987
                  Developed new distribution outlets through cold-
                  calls and follow-up visits. Increased
                  distribution in my district by 45% over a three-
                  year period. Coordinated a direct mail program
                  that increased magazine subscriptions 120%.

                  Canon Co., Atlanta, GA
                  Sales representative, 1975 -1980
                  Sold and serviced office copiers to businesses and
                  schools in the greater Atlanta area. Maintained
                  good customer relations through frequent calls and
                  visits. Identified potential customers.

EDUCATION: Atlanta University, Atlanta, GA
                  B.S. in Communications, 1974

PROFESSIONAL
MEMBERSHIPS: National Association of Importers
                  Rogers Park Community Association
                  Lion's Club

REFERENCES: Available on request.

JULIUS T. SHATTACK
45 E. 45th St. #414
Minneapolis, MN 50290
612/555-3490
612/555-8080

JOB OBJECTIVE

A position as a sales/marketing representative for a manufacturer of musical instruments.

PROFESSIONAL ACHIEVEMENTS

Sales

*Established and maintained an excellent relationship with over 100 accounts in the musical instrument industry.
*Resolved customer complaints promptly.
*Provided customers with detailed information on products and replacement parts.
*Named salesperson of the month six times.

Marketing

*Demonstrated the value of quantity purchases to customers.
*Researched industry competition to refine selling techniques.
*Projected success of new products through surveys and questionnaires.

WORK HISTORY

Roland Corporation, Minneapolis, MN
Sales Representative, 1987 - present

Twin Cities Electronics, St. Paul, MN
Salesperson, 1984 - 1987

EDUCATION

Milton Community College, Edina, MN
1982 - 1984

Elburn High School, St. Olaf, MN
Graduated 1982

REFERENCES

Available upon request

KENNETH THOMAS PARKER

1400 N. LAKE SHORE DRIVE
CHICAGO, IL 60601
312/555-1212 (DAY)
312/555-2901 (NIGHT)

JOB OBJECTIVE

Sales Manager for a company that manufactures sporting goods.

PROFESSIONAL EXPERIENCE

Sales and Promotion

* Made cold calls and visits to sporting goods retailers which resulted in increased accounts.
* Visited and serviced existing accounts to encourage continued sales.
* Advised customers on options available to meet a wide range of product needs.
* Handled dealer requests for information and sample products.

Marketing

* Researched competitive products in order to evaluate competitors' strengths and weaknesses.
* Planned a marketing strategy that resulted in a significant increase in accounts.
* Maintained demographic data in order to ascertain buyer profile.

EMPLOYMENT HISTORY

Wilson Sporting Goods, Inc., Morton Grove, IL
Assistant Sales Manager, 1985 - present
Sales Representative, 1983 - 1985

Chambers & Co., Chicago, IL
Marketing Assistant, 1982

Morey Mages Sporting Goods, Skokie, IL
Salesperson, 1980 - 1982

Bennigan's Restaurant, Lincolnwood, IL
Waiter, 1979 - 1980

KENNETH THOMAS PARKER - 2

EDUCATION

University of Illinois at Chicago, Chicago, IL
B.A. in Marketing, 1982

HONORS

Phi Beta Kappa, 1982
Honor Roll, 1980 - 1982
Seymour G. Reim Marketing Scholarship Recipient, 1980, 1981
President, Student Activities Board, 1982

SPECIAL SKILLS

Experience using a variety of word processing, data base and
spreadsheet software. Familiar with IBM and APPLE hardware.

REFERENCES

Provided on request

IRA T. SIMPSON
76 N. Washington Blvd.
Houston, TX   72009
714/555-4890

OBJECTIVE: A position as a sales representative which
involves direct sales and account management.

WORK
EXPERIENCE: R&G Sugar, Inc., Houston, TX
Salesman, 1987 - 1990
Sold refined sugar products to retail businesses.
Named top salesman of 1986. Maintained good
customer relations by identifying customer needs.
Trained new sales representatives and advised them
on effective selling techniques.

Popson Camera Co., Milwaukee, WI
Salesman, 1982 - 1987
Sold cameras to retail outfits in the South
suburban Milwaukee area. Increased territory
sales by 85% in five years. Demonstrated and
planned specific uses for products in various
offices. Maintained constant contact with
accounts.

EDUCATION: Popson Sales Training Course, Milwaukee, WI
Summer 1982

Cobert Technical High School, West Allis, WI
Graduated 1981
Football Team, Co-captain

REFERENCES: Available upon request

LINDA S. WOODS
3302 Harbor Drive South
#4554
Ft. Lauderdale, FL 33020
305/555-8903
305/555-9000

WORK EXPERIENCE

South Florida Boat Co., Miami, FL
District Sales Manager, 1986 - present

Planned successful strategies to identify and develop new accounts.
Increased sales by at least 20% each year (45% in 1988). Researched
and analyzed market conditions in order to seek out new customers.
Developed weekly and monthly sales strategies. Supervised seven
sales representatives.

Miami Frieght, Inc., Miami, FL
Account Executive, 1984 - 1986

Handled sales accounts for southern Florida area. Expanded customer
base by 25% during my tenure. Conducted field visits to solve
customer complaints. Maintained daily contact with customers by
telephone in order to insure good customer/company relations. Wrote
product information fliers and distributed them through a direct mail
plan.

Harrison Pandy, Inc., Denver, CO
Sales Representative, 1983 - 1984

Sold and serviced office copiers to businesses and school in the
greater Denver area. Maintained good customer relations through
frequent contact. Indentified potential customers for management.

EDUCATION

University of Colorado, Boulder, CO
B.A., 1983
Major: Economics
Minor: Music
G.P.A. 3.3/4.0

PROFESSIONAL MEMBERSHIPS

South Florida Sales Association, Treasurer, 1988 - 1990
Miami Chamber of Commerce, 1986 - present

REFERENCES

Available on request

IVAN P. LINS
24 E. Saginaw
Crystal Lake, IL 60203
708/555-3894

JOB OBJECTIVE

A position as a marketing manager where I can utilize my knowledge and
experience in sales and marketing.

RELEVANT ACCOMPLISHMENTS

* Managed sales of all product lines in midwestern markets for a leading maker
  of textiles.
* Represented five corporate divisions of the company with sales in excess of
  $3 million annually.
* Directed and motivated a sales force of 12 sales representatives in planned
  selling toward specific goals.
* Built wholesale and dealer distribution substantially as District Manager.
* Handled both internal and external areas of sales and marketing for an
  office supply manufacturer.
* Oversaw all aspects of samples, advertising and marketing.
* Maintained good customer relations with retail stores.

EMPLOYMENT HISTORY

ROBEAU INDUSTRIES, Chicago, IL
Regional Sales Manager, 1985 - present

CAROLINA CO., Elgin, IL
District Manager, 1980 - 1985

SUPER OFFICE SUPPLY, INC., St. Louis, MO
Assistant to the Sales Manager, 1976 - 1980

EDUCATION

UNIVERSITY OF MICHIGAN, Ann Arbor, MI
B.A. in Business Administration, 1975
Major: Marketing
Minor: Spanish

SEMINARS

National Management Association Seminar, 1984
Chicago University Seminars, 1987 - 1990

PROFESSIONAL MEMBERSHIPS

Sales and Marketing Association of Chicago
National Association of Market Developers

References available on request

JEFFREY CROSS

4901 Main St. #242
Evanston, IL 60202

JOB OBJECTIVE

Seeking a position as manager of a housewares department of a major
department store where I can use my talents as a manager and a
salesperson.

ACHIEVEMENTS

Promoted from customer service representive to salesperson to assistant
manager in housewares at Marshall Field's. Managed a staff of five,
including hiring, job training and supervision. Helped to reorganize
inventory control methods. Assisted customers in choosing housewares
and in interior design matters. Combined managerial and sales talents
to increase department sales figures.

WORK EXPERIENCE

Marshall Field's, Skokie, IL

Assistant Manager, 1989 - present
Salesperson, 1987 - 1989
Customer Service Representative, 1986 - 1987

Peters Hardware, Evanston, IL

Stock Clerk, Summers 1984 -1986

EDUCATION

Evanston High School, Evanston, IL
Graduated June 1986
Top 25% of class.
Student Council Representative
Animal Rights Committee

Oakton Community College, Des Plaines, IL
Various night courses, including "Sales Techniques" and "Retail Management"

AHA Seminar, "Selling Housewares," 1989

REFERENCES

Provided upon request

JANE WIGGINS

1814 N. Seminola Ave.
#2442
Cleveland, OH 47889
216/555-3400 (Daytime)
216/555-2910 (Evenings)

CAREER OBJECTIVE

To become a sales representative for an office supplies manufacturer.

EMPLOYMENT HISTORY

Tempo Office Supply Co., Cleveland, OH
Executive Secretary to Sales Manager, 1985 - present

Assisted the sales manager in various office activities and procedures.
Handled price quotations, information on product line, customer inquiries
on shipments and special orders. Arranged travel and transportation,
hotel, and scheduling of seminars and meetings. Drafted monthly reports
on sales procedures and profit margins. Managed computerization of the
office records.

James Plastics, St. Louis, MO
Secretary to Manager of Publications, 1983 - 1985

Arranged conferences for the department. Dealt directly with staff
members in a variety of manners including routing editing duties and
proofreading responsibilities. Edited and proofread inter-office memos
and a weekly department newsletter. Arranged for printing and distribution.
Supervised two student interns.

EDUCATION

Cleveland University, Cleveland, OH
B.S. in Marketing, 1987 (Evening Division)

St. Louis School of Business, St. Louis, MO
Completed advanced secretarial course, 1982

SPECIAL SKILLS

Proficiency on IBM and COMPAQ hardware and WORD PERFECT, DISPLAYWRITE and
MULTIMATE software. Knowledge of Spanish.

REFERENCES

Available on request

REBA MALONEY

331 Maple Ave.
Seattle, WA 99449

206/555-3893 (Home)   206/555-4444 (Work)

OBJECTIVE

A management position at a dress shop.

WORK EXPERIENCE

AVON DRESS SHOP, Seattle, WA
Assistant Sales Manager, 1989 - present

Sold dresses, waited on customers, advised on style, handled
special orders and mail orders and took care of returned
merchandise. Assisted in the design of window displays.
Oversaw the placement of ads for a major advertising campaign.
Represented store at conventions.

QUALITY BOUTIQUE, Tall Oaks, WA
Salesperson, 1987 - 1988

Sold accessories to customers, filled special orders, organized
and arranged inventory. Handled customer returns and special
requests. Designed window displays.

EDUCATION

TALL OAKS HIGH SCHOOL, Tall Oaks, WA

Graduated June 1988
Ranked 14 in a class of 300
Worked in student bookstore four years
Tennis Team

REFERENCES

Provided on request

EUNICE T. BODEANE
1221 E. Cambridge Ave.
Lynn, MA 02129
617/555-8800
617/555-9922

OBJECTIVE: A position as publicist with an arts organization.

WORK
EXPERIENCE: Boston Opera Co., Boston, MA
                  P.R. Assistant, 1986 - present
                  Composed press releases and public service announcements
                  which publicized Opera events. Developed contacts with
                  Boston entertainment columnists which resulted in extensive
                  coverage. Organized a calendar of advertising deadlines.
                  Wrote ad copy for print and radio media.

                  Sandra Watt Agency, Boston, MA
                  Editorial/P.R. Assistant, 1981 - 1986
                  Edited technical and literary manuscripts. Compiled a
                  directory of Boston editors and publishers for agency use.
                  Organized an educational workshop for local writers.

EDUCATION: Ithica University, Ithica, NY
                  B.S. in Advertising, 1980
                  Coursework included: Marketing Techniques, Advertising,
                  Corporate Public Relations, P.R. Techniques.

HONORS: Sigma Kappa Nu Honorary Society
                  Honors in Advertising
                  Dean's List
                  Myron T. Kapp Public Relations Award

ACTIVITIES: Student Government Representative
                  Homecoming Committee
                  Soccer Club

SPECIAL
SKILLS: Proficient on IBM hardware and Word Perfect 5 software.
                  Fluent in Italian.

                  REFERENCES PROVIDED IF NEEDED

WINONA T. SIMPSON
420 W. Easterly Avenue
Indianapolis, IN 49091
317/555-1212

OBJECTIVE

A management position in marketing or public relations.

PROFESSIONAL ACHIEVEMENTS

Marketing/Public Relations

* Developed a successful marketing campaign for a video rental chain.
* Initiated and maintained a positive working relationship with radio and print media.
* Implemented marketing strategies to increase sales at less profitable stores.
* Designed a training program for store managers and staff.

Promotion

* Demonstrated electronic equipment in stereo and department stores.
* Reported customer reactions to manufacturers.
* Designed fliers and advertising to promote products.
* Made frequent calls to retail outlets.

EMPLOYMENT HISTORY

Blockbuster Video, Inc., Indianapolis, IN
P.R. Director, 1985 - present

Jeron Stereo, Bloomington, IN
Marketing Representative, 1982 - 1985

Kader Advertising, St. Louis, MO
P.R. Assistant, 1980 - 1982

EDUCATION

Washington University, St. Louis, MO
B.S. in Education, 1980

HONORS

Phi Beta Kappa, 1980
Top 5% of class
Dean's List

REFERENCES

Provided on request

STEVEN TYLER

17001 E. Riverside Dr.   818/555-3728 (Day)
Burbank, CA 91505   818/555-9000 (Night)

OBJECTIVE

Marketing management.

RELEVANT ACHIEVEMENTS

Marketing

* Implemented various promotional programs including product, visuals, giveaways,
  visuals and delivery of presentation.
* Conceived and developed creative product promotions.
* Designed unique advertising with innovative placements, including billboards,
  trade publications and newspapers.
* Administered advertising budget.
* Represented company to both industry and media.

Sales

* Exceed revenue goals by 41% this last year.
* Set annual sales records in 1987 with revenues of $55 million.
* Administered a $125 million advertising budget.

Management

* Restructured Paradise Vacations achieving #1 position in sales for the western
  U.S.
* Designed and wrote new policy manuals and job descriptions for all departments.
* Trained staff and managers in order to increase productivity.
* Directed the sales force in achieving and exceeding sales goals.

EMPLOYMENT HISTORY

Paradise Vacations, Burbank, CA
Senior Vice President, 1986 - present
Vice President, Sales and Marketing, 1985 - 1986

Western Airlines, San Diego, CA
Vice President of Sales, 1983 - 1985
Director, Sales Department, 1980 - 1983

SAS Airlines, Los Angeles, CA
Regional Sales Manager, 1975 - 1980
District Sales Manager, 1971 - 1975

TWA, Houston, TX
Sales Representative, 1966 - 1971

Steven Tyler - 2

<u>United Plastics, Inc.</u>, Beverly Glen, CA
Sales Representative, 1959 - 1964

EDUCATION

<u>Colorado University</u>, Denver, CO
M.B.A., 1966
Graduated with honors

<u>Revers College</u>, Beaver Falls, KY
B.S. in Communications, 1958

SEMINARS

International Sales and Marketing
Domestic Sales and Marketing
Management and Administration
Travel Sales Incentives
Telemarketing

REFERENCES

Available on request

GINA CAROL STONE
5001 Lincoln Drive #2
Marlton, NJ 08053
609/555-1200
609/555-3893

OBJECTIVE: Sales manager of a paper products company.

PROFESSIONAL
EXPERIENCE: HARRISON PAPER CO., Philadelphia, PA
                District Sales Manager, 1984 - 1990

                Planned successful strategies in order to identify and
                develop new accounts. Increased sales by at least 20%
                each year (50% in 1988). Researched and analyzed market
                conditions in order to seek out new customers. Developed
                weekly and monthly sales strategies. Supervised seven
                sales representatives.

                DANIEL P. MILLER & CO., Trenton, NJ
                Sales Representative, 1977 - 1984

                Developed and managed new territories. Built sales through
                calls on retailers and wholesalers. Developed creative
                techniques for increasing product sales. Maintained current
                knowledge of competitive products. Wrote weekly and
                monthly sales reports.

                SAMMY'S BEST BURGER CO., Newark, NJ
                Assistant to Sales Manager, 1970 - 1977

                Handled both internal and external areas of sales and
                marketing, including samples, advertising and pricing.
                Served as company sales representative and sold a variety
                of products to retail stores.

EDUCATION: NEW JERSEY STATE UNIVERSITY, Trenton, NJ
                B.A. in Botany, 1969
                Graduated in top 10% of class
                Recipient of Floyd T. Harper Botany Scholarship

SPECIAL
SKILLS: Programming experience in Basic and Fortran. Software
                programs used: Wordstar, Webase 2, Appleworks. Working
                knowledge of Russian.

REFERENCES: Available on request.

WILLIAM ROBERT GARRETT
5050 W. Palatine Road
Palatine, IL   60067
708/555-3789 (Home)
708/555-1000 (Work)

JOB OBJECTIVE

A management level position in computer sales where I can utilize my
sales and technical experience in the computer industry.

RELEVANT EXPERIENCE

Sales

* Handled sales accounts for northwest suburban Chicago area.
* Expanded customer base by 25% during my tenure.
* Conducted field visits to solve customers problems.
* Maintained daily contact with customers to insure good customer/company
  relations.
* Wrote product information fliers and sales manual.

Technical

* Installed and maintained operating system.
* Defined and oversaw network lists and tables.
* Coordinated problem solving with phone companies.
* Performance tuned subsystems and networks.
* Planned and installed new hardware and programming techiniques

Systems Analysis

* Documented procedures for mechanization of payroll department.
* Created standards and procedures for main accounting system.
* Coordinated requirements meeting with production department on new
  inventory system.
* Developed test procedures for reverification of new application.
* Developed distribution lists, user IDs and standards for electronic
  mail system.

EMPLOYMENT HISTORY

MICROTECH COMPUTERS, Northbrook, IL
Account Executive, 1979 - present

APPLE COMPUTERS, Berkeley, CA
Technical Support Specialist, 1972 - 1979

DATALOG, INC., St. Louis, MO
Systems Analyst, 1961 - 1971

William Robert Garrett - 2

EDUCATION

UNIVERSITY OF CHICAGO, Chicago, IL
M.S. in Mathematics, 1959
Honors graduate

Northwestern University, Evanston, IL
B.S. in Communications, 1956

PROFESSIONAL AFFILIATIONS

Computer Sales Association
Illinois Business Chapter
Citizens for a Cleaner Environment

SEMINARS

Microtech Sales Seminars
Apple Technical Workshops

REFERENCES AVAILABLE ON REQUEST

HARRIET SCHUMACHER

1414 N. Montebello Drive
Berkeley, CA   98028
415/555-4930

EDUCATION:	<u>University of California at Berkeley</u> Bachelor of Science in Marketing Expected June 1991
HONORS:	Beta Gamma Upsilon Honorary Society Dean's list Manley Writing Award, 1989
ACTIVITIES:	Treasurer, Gamma Gamma Gamma Sorority Freshman Advisor Homecoming Planning Committee Alumni Welcoming Committee
WORK EXPERIENCE:	<u>AT&T</u>, New York, NY Marketing Intern, 1990 Assisted marketing staff in the areas of research, demographics, sales forecasts, identifying new customers and promotion. <u>University of California at Berkeley</u> Office Assistant, Journalism School, 1988-1990 Assisted with registrations, filing and typing. Arranged application materials. Assembled course packs.
SPECIAL SKILLS:	Fluent in German. Hands-on computer experience using LOTUS 123 and dBASE III.
REFERENCES:	Available on request.

PATRICK H. McCOY
1701 N. Hampshire Pl.
Miami, FL 03908
305/555-3909
305/555-9099

OBJECTIVE: A position as a sales manager for a furnace manufacturer.

WORK
EXPERIENCE: NEWMARK FURNACE CO., Miami, FL
                Account Executive, 1987 - present

                Handled sales accounts for southern Florida area. Expanded
                customer base by 28% during my tenure. Conducted field visits
                to solve customer complaints. Maintained daily contact with
                customers to insure good company/customer relations. Wrote
                product information fliers and distributed them to potential
                customers.

                POTISCO, Terre Haute, IN
                Sales Representative, 1983 - 1987

                Handled sales to customers, particularly contractors. Priced
                bid estimates as required. Oversaw customer and public relations
                which helped to build company's image. Set up office procedures
                where necessary.

                HONOCO, INC., Chicago, IL
                Sales Representative, 1980 - 1983

                Developed and managed new territories. Built sales by calls
                on physicians, hospitals, retailers and wholesalers. Developed
                creative techniques for increasing product sales. Maintained
                current knowledge of competitive products.

EDUCATION: WHEATON COLLEGE, Wheaton, IL
                B.A. in Business, 1979

SEMINARS: Sales and Marketing in the 80s
                Florida Business Association
                Marketing for the Furnace Industry

REFERENCES: Available on request.

GERALD ROBERT SCAMPI

4890 W. 57th St.
New York, NY 10019
212/555-3678

JOB OBJECTIVE

A position as a marketing and promotion manager where I can
utilize my experience and special skills.

PROFESSIONAL
EXPERIENCE

1983-1987 ATLANTIC RECORDS, New York, NY
Promotion Manager. Developed and executed all marketing
strategy for record promotion in New York, New Jersey and
Massachussetts. Interfaced with sales department and retail
stores to insure adequate product placement. Attended various
company sponsered sales, marketing and management seminars.

1973-1982 RSO RECORDS, Miami, FL
Promotion Manager. Planned all marketing strategy for record
promotions in the southeast U.S. Worked closely with sales and
touring bands to insure product visibility in the marketplace.

1971-1973 WCFL RADIO, Chicago, IL
Served as a morning DJ. Played CHR music. Made TV appearances
and public events appearances for the station. Organized and
staffed station's news department. Promoted to Music Director
after one year.

1966-1971 WGLT RADIO, Atlanta, GA
Served as Program Director, Music Director and News Director
during my tenure.

EDUCATION

COLUMBIA COLLEGE, Chicago, IL
Attended 1965 -1966
Studied Audio Engineering

References available on request

DANIEL KEYS

548 W. Hollywood Way
Burbank, CA 91505
818/555-9090

PROFESSIONAL OBJECTIVE:

An upper-level management position in the record industry where I can
employ my sales, marketing and promotion experience.

PROFESSIONAL BACKGROUND:

Warner Bros. Records, Burbank, CA
Director of Marketing/Jazz Department, 1988 - present
Developed and implemented strategic marketing plans for new releases and
catalog. Produced reissue packages and samplers, both retail and
promotional. Created ad copy. Interfaced with creative services and
national/local print & radio. Oversaw all aspects of sales. Coordinated
promotional activities and chart reports.

I.R.S. Records, Los Angeles, CA
National Sales Manager, 1984 - 1988
West Coast Sales Manager, 1981 - 1984
Increased sales profile specifically west coast retailers, one-stops and
racks. Promoted to National Sales Manager where I established sales
and promotion programs for the company. Coordinated radio/chart reports.

Specialty Records, Scranton, PA
Sales Representative, 1980
Handled sales, merchandising and account servicing for LPs and cassettes.
Called on major chains and small independent retailers. Promoted new
releases and maintained account inventory.

Tower Records, Los Angeles, CA
Manager, 1979 - 1980
Handled sales, merchandising, customer service, product selection and ordering,
personnel management and supervision for a full line retail outlet.

MCA Records Distribution, Universal City, CA
Sales Representative, 1973 - 1979
Promoted and sold MCA product to Los Angeles and surrounding counties.
Designed in-store and window displays. Coordinated media advertising
support programs.

EDUCATION:

Berkeley University, Berkeley, CA
B.A., Liberal Arts, 1971

References provided on request

DONALD R. CRUMP

5001 Providence St.   201/555-8000
Washington, D.C.   02930   201/555-3894

OBJECTIVE: A position as marketing manager for Graphics, Inc.

PROFESSIONAL
EXPERIENCE: Burger World, Inc., Washington, D.C.
                Marketing Director, 1983 - 1990
                Developed a successful marketing campaign for a fast food
                chain. Initiated and maintained a positive working relationship
                with radio, T.V. and print media. Implemented marketing
                strategies to increase sales at less profitable outlets.
                Designed a training program for store managers and staff.

                Hi Fidelity Stereo Co., Newark, NJ
                Marketing Representative, 1978 - 1983
                Demonstrated electronic equipment in stereo and department
                stores. Reported customer reactions to manufacturers.
                Designed fliers and advertising to promote products. Made
                frequent calls to retail outlets.

                Interco, New York, NY
                Sales Representative, 1971 - 1978
                Identified clients' needs and problems and assured them of
                personal attention. Resolved service and billing prcblems.
                Delivered sales presentations to groups and individuals.
                Identified potential customers and established new accounts.

EDUCATION: Georgetown University, Washington, D.C.
                B.S. Evening Division, 1977
                Major: Marketing
                Minor: English

SEMINARS: Washington Sales and Marketing Convention, 1988, 1989
                National Marketing Association Seminar, 1980 - 1985

SPECIAL
SKILLS: Fluent in Spanish. Able to program in BASIC.

REFERENCES: Available on request

MATTHEW R. CLARKSON

1251 S. Maple Ave.
Des Moines, IA 52909
515/555-4999 (Day)
515/555-3429 (Evening)

OBJECTIVE: Manager of the hardware department of a major department store.

RELEVANT
ACHIEVEMENTS: * Promoted from customer service representative to salesperson and
                then to assistant manager in hardware at Sears in Des Moines.

              * Managed a staff of six, including hiring, job training and
                supervision.

              * Helped to reorganize inventory control methods.

              * Assisted customers in choosing and using hardware products.

              * Combined managerial and sales talents to increase department
                sales.

EMPLOYMENT
HISTORY: Sears, Des Moines, IA

                 Assistant Manager, 1988 - present
                 Salesperson, 1986 - 1988
                 Customer Service Representative, 1985 - 1986

                 Sam's Hardware, West Petersville, IA

                 Stock Clerk, Summers 1983 - 1985

EDUCATION: Des Moines Township High School, Des Moines, IA
                 Graduated June 1985
                 Top 25% of class.
                 Student Council Secretary
                 Homecoming Committee

                 Redbrook College, Des Moines, IA
                 Various night courses, including "Retail Sales Management" and
                 "Supervisory Techniques."

REFERENCES: Available on request

SALLY JOHANSON
3240 Santa Monica Blvd.
Los Angeles, CA 90028
213/555-9832 (Home)
213/555-2121 (Work)

OBJECTIVE

A position as an assistant sales manager for automobile manufacturer.

SKILLS AND ACCOMPLISHMENTS

Sales

Identified clients' needs and problems and assured them of personal attention.
Resolved service and billing problems.
Delivered sales presentations to groups and individuals.
Identified potential new clients and established new accounts.
Increased client base by 40%.

Development

Orchestrated market analyses and researched competition for reports to the
district manager.
Prepared sales forecasts and sales goals reports.
Developed monthly sales plans which identified necessary account maintenance
and specific problems that required attention.
Maintained daily sales logs and referral logs.

EMPLOYMENT HISTORY

Yugo America, Inc., Los Angeles, CA
Sales Representative, 1988 - present

Trak Autoparts, Inc., Burbank, CA
Sales Representative, 1985 - 1988

Apple One Temporary, Glendale, CA
Sales Representative, 1984 - 1985

McDonalds Corp., Jos Angeles, CA
Management Trainee, 1984

EDUCATION

Burbank College of Art, Burbank, CA
B.A. in Art, 1984

REFERENCES

Available on request

THEODORE WELLINGTON
34 W. Washington Drive
New York, NY 10019
212/555-4904

JOB OBJECTIVE

A senior management position in sales and marketing.

RELEVANT ACHIEVEMENTS

* Introduced new and existing product lines through presentations to
  marketing directors.
* Developed new products which resulted in increased sales.
* Increased sales from $3 million to $12 million during the past six
  years.
* Supervised five sales agencies throughout the U.S. and Canada.
* Developed fifteen new accounts.
* Researched the market in order to coordinate product line with
  current trends.
* Increased company's share of the market through improved quality products.

EMPLOYMENT HISTORY

Surf City Skateboard Co., New York, NY
Vice President of Sales and Marketing, 1979 - present

Nike, Inc., San Bernadino, CA
Sales and Product Manager, 1974 - 1979

Vons Ltd., Los Angeles, CA
Sales Representative, 1969 - 1974

EDUCATION

University of Southern California, Los Angeles, CA
B.S. in Marketing, 1968

SEMINARS

Manhattan Sales & Marketing Seminar, 1987 - 1990
National Marketing Association, 1982 - 1986

REFERENCES

Provided on request

JAMES ROBERT WEITSMA

1200 Wodler Drive
Apartment 3E
Chicago, IL 60607   Telephone: 312/555-4903

OBJECTIVE: A position as a sales management trainee.

EDUCATION: NORTHWESTERN UNIVERSITY, Evanston, IL

                B.A. in Advertising, 1990
                Dean's List five quarters
                3.21 GPA in major field
                3.07 GPA overall
                Alumni Committee
                Student Activities Board

                CENTRAL HIGH SCHOOL, Chicago, IL

                Graduated 1986
                Top 15% of class
                Vice President of Senior Class
                Editor of Student Newspaper
                Student Government
                Tennis Team

WORK
EXPERIENCE: AT&T, Chicago, IL
                Sales Intern, 1989
                Assisted sales manager in areas of promotion, product
                development and marketing.

                HANDELMAN MARKETING, Winnetka, IL
                Telephone Surveyor, Summer 1987 - 1988

                YESTERDAY'S, Evanston, IL
                Waiter, Summer 1986

SPECIAL
SKILLS: Fluent in Spanish. Familiar with various computer software
                and hardware.

REFERENCES: Available on request

YOSHEMA MUNO
7640 N. Redden Road
Skokie, IL 60076
708/555-3908
708/555-2300

JOB OBJECTIVE

A position as manager of a store that sells quality shoes and accessories.

WORK EXPERIENCE

Florsheim Shoes, Skokie, IL
Assistant Manager, 1987 - 1990

Served as assistant manager of a quality shoe store with partial supervision of eight salespeople. Researched customers' buying habits and preferences. Handled promotion and mailings for special sales and in-store events. Helped to increase sales through personal attention to customer needs.

Handleman Shoe Store, Lincolnwood, IL
Salesperson, 1983 - 1987

Sold high-quality women's shoes at an exclusive store. Named top salesperson of 1986 & 1987. Maintained a clean, attractive store area and organized inventory.

Florsheim Shoes, Chicago, IL
Salesperson, 1980 - 1983

Sold shoes. Assisted customers in making purchase decisions. Organized and maintained stock and inventory. Helped with window displays.

EDUCATION

Stevenson Community College, Chicago, IL
Attended two years. Majored in Political Science.

Calumet High School, Calumet, IL
Graduated 1980. Won Science Award.

REFERENCES

Available on request

DARREN TREVOL
43433 N. Melrose Ave.
Elmhurst, IL   60189
708/555-4328
708/555-1010

OBJECTIVE: Senior vice president of sales and marketing
                    Vincent Electronics, Inc.

PROFESSIONAL
ACHIEVEMENTS:

                    Marketing

                    * Researched computer market in order to
                    coordinate product line with current public
                    tastes and buying trends.
                    * Developed new approaches to marketing software
                      products, including in-store displays and
                    advertising.
                    * Organized and planned convention displays and
                      strategies.

                    Sales

                    * Introduced new and existing product lines
                      through presentations to major clients.
                    * Increased sales from $27 million to $50 million
                      in five years.
                    * Initiated and developed nine new accounts.
                    * Supervised five sales agencies throughout the
                      U.S.

EMPLOYMENT
HISTORY: Vincent Electronics Co., Elmhurst, IL
                    Sales and Marketing Manager, 1985 - present

                    Porcelana Inc., Melrose Park, IL
                    Product Coordinator, 1980 - 1985

                    Radio Shack, Inc., New York, NY
                    Sales Representative, 1975 - 1980

EDUCATION: New York University, New York, NY
                    B.S. 1975
                    Major: Business Administration
                    Minor: Computer Science

REFERENCES: Available upon request

JUAN C. GARCIA
2103 AFTON STREET
TEMPLE HILL, MARYLAND 20748
HOME (301) 555-2419

EDUCATION: Columbia University, New York, NY
                      Majors: Business, Philosophy
                      Degree expected: Bachelor of Arts, 1990
                      Grade point average: 3.0
                      Regents Scholarship recipient
                      Columbia University Scholarship recipient

EXPERIENCE:

7/89-9/89   Graduate Business Library, Columbia University, NY
                      General library duties. Entered new students and
                      books onto computer files. Gave out microfiche.
                      Reserved and distributed materials.

9/88-5/89   German Department, Columbia University, NY
                      Performed general office duties. Offered extensive
                      information assistance by phone and in person.
                      Collated and proofread class materials. Assisted
                      professors in the gathering of class materials.

6/88-9/88   Loan Collections Department, Columbia University, NY
                      Initiated new filing system for the office. Checked
                      arrears in Bursar's Office during registration period.

9/87-5/88   School of Continuing Education, Columbia University, NY
                      Involved in heavy public contact as well as general
                      clerical duties.

SPECIAL ABILITIES: Total fluency in Spanish. Currently studying German.
                      Can program in BASIC. Excellent research skills.

REFERENCES: Available on request

LISA STANSFIELD

14 E. ThreePenny Road
Detroit, MI 33290
313/555-3489

OBJECTIVE

A management position in marketing where I can utilize my
promotion and public relations experience.

WORK EXPERIENCE

SEVEN ELEVEN INC., Detroit, MI
Marketing Director, 1986 - present
Developed a successful marketing campaign for a convenience store
chain. Initiated and maintained a positive working relationship
with radio and print media. Implemented marketing strategies to
increase sales at less profitable outlets. Designed a training
program for store managers and staff.

SUPER VACUUM CO., Bloomfield Hills, MI
Marketing Representative, 1982 -1986
Demonstrated vacuums in specialty and department stores.
Reported customer reactions to manufacturers. Designed fliers
and advertising to promote products. Made frequent calls to
retail outlets.

REBO CARPETS, INC., Chicago, IL
Assistant to Sales Manager, 1977 - 1982
Handled both internal and external areas of sales and marketing,
including samples, advertising and pricing. Served as company
sales representative and sold carpeting to retail outlets.

EDUCATION

UNIVERSITY OF MICHIGAN, Ann Arbor, MI
B.A. Marketing, 1976

SEMINARS

Michigan Marketing Workshop, 1988, 1989
Sales and Marketing Association Seminars, 1984

References available on request.

RESUME

CAROL GHERKIN   Telephones: (612) 555-4342
4432 W. Simpson St.   (612) 555-4000
Minneapolis, MN 44515

JOB OBJECTIVE:

Seeking a sales position with a pharmaceutical company that services hospitals
where I can utilize my education, my communication skills and my sales
experience.

EMPLOYMENT EXPERIENCE:

Sales Representative, Pharmamed, Inc, St. Paul, MN, 1988 to present.
Demonstrated and explained new drugs to physicians. Handled follow-ups
and updates on previous product. Increased sales 30% in my first two years.
Helped to train new sales representatives.

Sales Trainee, Hospo Supply Co., Edina, MN, 1987.
Determined which drugs were necessary for stocking hospital supply rooms.
Handled stocking for previously established orders. Increased staff awareness
of new products.

EDUCATION:

M.S., University of Minnesota, Chemistry, 1987
B.S., Iowa State University, Biology, 1985

SEMINARS:

"Presenting New Drugs To In-Office Physicians," SMPA, 1987

HONORS:

Raymond Johnson Chemistry Award, 1987
Phi Beta Kappa, 1985
Dean's List, 1984, 1985

ACTIVITIES:

Chemistry Club, 1987
Biology Club, 1984-1985

References available on request

CARLOS ENRIQUE PENA

14 E. Bryn Mawr Ave.
Chicago, IL 60645
312/555-3849

JOB OBJECTIVE: A position as vice president of sales at
                  Florsheim Shoe Co.

PROFESSIONAL
EXPERIENCE: Florsheim Shoe Co., Chicago, IL
                  Sales Manager, 1985 - present
                  Sold custom designed point-of-purchase
                  elements and product displays. Researched
                  target areas and developed new account leads.
                  Researched and determined advertising in
                  national publications. Made sales
                  presentations to potential customers.
                  Participated in plastics industry trade
                  shows.

                  Quest Fixtures, Inc., St. Louis, MO
                  District Sales Manager, 1981 - 1985
                  Planned successful sales strategies in order
                  to identify and develop new accounts.
                  Supervised seven sales representatives.
                  Increased sales by at least 20% in each of my
                  four years. Researched and analyzed market
                  conditions to seek out new customers. Wrote
                  monthly sales reports.

                  Carolina Freight Co., Raleigh, NC
                  Account Executive, 1978 - 1981
                  Managed accounts in the greater Raleigh area.
                  Expanded customer base 30% in four years.
                  Maintained daily contact with customers by
                  telephone in order to insure good
                  customer/company relations. Wrote product
                  information fliers and distributed them
                  through a direct mail program.

EDUCATION: Boston University, Boston, MA
                  M.B.A. with honors, 1977

                  Western University, Phoenix, AZ
                  B.A. in Accounting, 1974

PROFESSIONAL
MEMBERSHIPS: Midwest Sales Association, 1986 - present
                  Midwest Merchants Group, 1981 - present

REFERENCES: Available upon request

JOHN L. RYDER

211 W. Fourth St. #211
Brooklyn, NY 10001
718/555-9080

JOB OBJECTIVE

Seeking a sales management position in a medium to large-sized insurance company.

ACCOMPLISHMENTS

Increased sales 17% the first year I sold group policies to businesses and unions. Sales increases have averaged 15% to 20% in subsequent years.

Chaired a committee which developed a sales manual which explained group insurance sales techniques.

Served as insurance adjustor for Brooklyn Health Co., a 20,000 member HMO.

Handled highly technical reimbursements by the state to the HMO.

Wrote and edited annual reports and quarterly reports.

Investigated and reported on adjustments and claims.

WORK EXPERIENCE

Interco Insurance Co., New York, NY
Insurance Agent, 1985 - present

Brooklyn Health Co., Brooklyn, NY
Health Insurance Adjustor, 1980 - 1985

City of St. Louis, St. Louis, MO
Claims Adjustor, 1975-1980

EDUCATION

M.B.A., Washington University, St. Louis, MO, 1974
B.A., Washington University, St. Louis, MO, 1972

SPECIAL ABILITIES

Extensive experience with various computer software and hardware, including word processing, data base and spreadsheet.

Willing to relocate and travel if necessary.

REFERENCES FURNISHED UPON REQUEST

GLORIA GARLAND

1220 Market St. #3   415/555-5508
San Francisco, CA   92299   415/555-5200

OBJECTIVE: A position as sales manager.

WORK
EXPERIENCE: <u>Sandler Imports</u>, Sausalito, CA
                 Sales Coordinator, 1987 - present
                 Managed ten field representatives. Handled
                 information dissemination and distribution. Co-
                 designed a full-color catalog. Placed advertising
                 in major trade publications. Promoted products at
                 trade shows. Maintained inventory status reports
                 and personnel records.

                 <u>Redwood Textbook Co.</u>, San Francisco, CA
                 Distribution Assistant, 1980 - 1987
                 Developed new distribution outlets through cold-
                 calls and follow-up visits. Increased
                 distribution in my district by 45% over a three-
                 year period. Coordinated a direct mail program
                 that increased magazine subscriptions 120%.

                 <u>Xerox Co.</u>, Atlanta, GA
                 Sales representative, 1975 -1980
                 Sold and serviced office copiers to businesses and
                 schools in the greater Atlanta area. Maintained
                 good customer relations through frequent calls and
                 visits. Identified potential customers.

EDUCATION: <u>Miami University</u>, Miami, OH
                 B.S. in Communications, 1974

PROFESSIONAL
MEMBERSHIPS: National Association of Importers
                 Sausalito Community Association
                 San Francisco Chamber of Commerce

REFERENCES: Available on request.

SCOTT JONES

612 E. Mayfair Road
Arlington Heights, IL   60005
312/555-6721 (Day)
312/555-9339 (Evening)

OBJECTIVE	A sales position in commercial real estate.
EXPERIENCE	ERA Realty, Inc., Arlington Heights, IL Domestic real estate salesperson, 1987 to present. Sold homes in the Northwest suburban area. Interacted with clients, real estate agents, brokers and bank personnel. Awarded ERA Northwest Suburban Salesperson of the year, 1989. Arlington Heights Camera Shop, Arlington Heights, IL Camera salesperson, 1982-1987 Sold cameras and film. Assisted customers in filling orders and repairs. Trained new members of sales staff. Reorganized inventory system.
PROFESSIONAL ACTIVITIES	Member, Northwest Suburban Realty Association, 1988 to present. Member, Arlington Heights Chamber of Commerce.
EDUCATION	University of Illinois at Chicago, 1986-1987 Major: Business Harper Community College, Palatine, IL 1985-1986
SPECIAL SKILLS	Proficient on WORD PERFECT 5 and LOTUS 1-2-3.
REFERENCES	Provided upon request

JAMES BROWN
12 HINMAN AVE. #3
ST. PAUL, MN 51111
612/555-6490
612/555-6565

JOB OBJECTIVE

A position as a marketing representative for a manufacturer of textiles.

PROFESSIONAL ACHIEVEMENTS

Marketing

*Demonstrated the value of quantity purchases to customers.
*Researched industry competition to refine selling techniques.
*Projected success of new products through surveys and questionnaires.

Sales

*Established and maintained an excellent relationship with over 100 accounts in the textile industry.
*Resolved customer complaints promptly.
*Provided customers with detailed information on product line.
*Named salesperson of the month six times.

WORK HISTORY

Rand Textiles, Inc., St. Paul, MN
Sales Representative, 1987 - present

St. Paul Woolen Products, St. Paul, MN
Salesperson, 1984 - 1987

EDUCATION

Oakton Community College, Pottersville, MN
1982 - 1984

St. Rose High School, St. Olaf, MN
Graduated 1982

REFERENCES

Available upon request

ELIZABETH TAMARA YOKEL
700 E. Terrapin Station #44
Philadelphia, PA 29920
219/555-8908.

OBJECTIVE: Sales representative for a travel-related company.

EXPERIENCE: Pan American Airlines, Philadelphia, PA
                  Sales representative, 1986 - present
                  Sold reservations for domestic flights, hotels and
                  car rentals. Marketed travel packages through
                  travel agencies. Negotiated airline and hotel
                  discounts for customers. Devised itineraries and
                  solved customers' travel related problems.

                  Sonia's Travel , Allentown, PA
                  Travel Agent, 1980 - 1986
                  Handled customer reservations for airlines,
                  hotels, and car rentals. Advised customers on
                  competitive travel packages and prices.
                  Interacted with all major airlines, hotel chains
                  and car rental companies.

EDUCATION: University of Wisconsin, Madison, WI
                  B.A. in English, 1956

SPECIAL
SKILLS: Hands-on experience using most travel-related
                  computer systems, including Sabre and Apollo.

                  Working knowledge of Russian.

REFERENCES: Available on request.

SANDRA L. PEARSON

12 E. Tenth St.
San Francisco, CA 94890
415/555-2343

JOB OBJECTIVE

A management position in cable television advertising sales.

RELEVANT EXPERIENCE

*Sold space in television for four major clients in the automotive industry.

*Served as a liaison between clients and television and radio station salespeople.

*Researched demographic and public buying habits for clients.

*Sold space for daytime programming on local T.V. station.

*Advised station on content and suitability of ads.

*Served as a liaison between station and those purchasing advertising space.

EMPLOYMENT HISTORY

Medialink Advertising Agency, San Francisco, CA
Television Space Sales, September 1985 - June 1990.

KTUT Television, Portland, OR
Television Space Sales, October 1983 - August 1985.

KFTF Radio, Berkeley, CA
Staff Sales Assistant, June 1981 - June 1983.

EDUCATION

B.A. in Communications, University of California at Berkeley, 1983.

HONORS

Seeger Award, Outstanding Communications Senior, 1983
Dean's List, five semesters
Salutatorian, Overland High School, Palo Alto, CA, 1979

REFERENCES PROVIDED ON REQUEST

JOHN JAMES HYMAN, III
5555 Euclid Avenue
Ft. Lauderdale, FL   33053
305/555-8982 (Day)
305/555-6001 (Evening)

OBJECTIVE: A sales management position with a machine tool manufacturer where
I can apply my abilities and experience in sales and marketing.

WORK
EXPERIENCE: Florida Hydraulics, Inc., Miami, FL
Assistant Sales Manager, January 1985 - present
Managed a staff of seven sales representatives. Supervised the
production of a marketing newsletter which has circulation throughout
the company. Co-wrote the annual marketing plan. Served as a
liaison between sales staff and upper management.

Peaston Machine Tools, Inc., Tampa, FL
Sales Representative, March 1982 - November 1984
Sold machine tools to business and industry. Wrote articles on
sales techniques for monthly newsletter. Handled seven accounts
in which sales rose 29% during my tenure.

EDUCATION: B.S. in Civil Engineering, Miami University, Miami, FL, 1981

PROFESSIONAL
MEMBERSHIPS: Society of Civil Engineers, New York, NY
1983 - present

Machine Tools Sales Organization, Chicago, IL
1984 - present

SPECIAL SKILLS: Fluent in Spanish and French.

REFERENCES: Available on request

MARK T. CHRISTENSON

65 W. Harrison
Minneapolis, MN 44490
612/555-1212 (DAY)
612/555-2901 (NIGHT)

JOB OBJECTIVE

Sales Manager for a company that manufactures computer software.

PROFESSIONAL EXPERIENCE

Sales and Promotion

* Made cold calls and visits to software retailers which resulted in increased accounts.
* Visited and serviced existing accounts to encourage continued sales.
* Advised customers on options available to meet a wide range of product needs.
* Handled dealer requests for information and sample products.

Marketing

* Researched competitive products in order to evaluate competitors' strengths and weaknesses.
* Planned a marketing strategy that resulted in a significant increase in accounts.
* Maintained demographic data in order to ascertain buyer profile.

EMPLOYMENT HISTORY

Thomas Software, Inc., Minneapolis, MN
Assistant Sales Manager, 1985 - present
Sales Representative, 1983 - 1985

Quaker & Co., St. Paul, MN
Marketing Assistant, 1982

USA Computer Supplies, Skokie, IL
Salesperson, 1980 - 1982

Bennigan's Restaurant, Columbus, OH
Waiter, 1979 - 1980

MARK T. CHRISTENSON - 2

EDUCATION

Washington University, St. Louis, MO
B.A. in Marketing, 1982

HONORS

Phi Beta Kappa, 1982
Honor Roll, 1980 - 1982
Terrance C. Maples Marketing Scholarship Recipient, 1980, 1981
President, Student Activities Board, 1982

SPECIAL SKILLS

Experience using a variety of word processing, data base and
spreadsheet software. Familiar with IBM and APPLE hardware.

REFERENCES

Provided on request

CAROL A. BADEN

Permanent Address: Temporary Address:
South East Hollow Road   150 Fort Washington Ave.
Berlin, NY 10951   New York, NY 10032
(518) 555-6057   (212) 738-2498

OBJECTIVE: A management trainee position in the telecommunications
                    industry.

EDUCATION: Bachelor of Science, Communications
                    New York University, New York, NY
                    Date of Graduation, May 1990
                    Communications G.P.A. 3.45
                    Academic G.P.A. 3.07

PROFESSIONAL
EXPERIENCE: V.I.T.A. (Volunteer Income Tax Assistance), Spring 1990
                    Provided income tax assistance to lower income and
                    elderly taxpayers who were unable to prepare returns or
                    pay for professional assistance.

                    Tutor, Self-employed, September 1988 - present
                    Helped students to better understand the basic concepts
                    and ideas mathematics.

                    Randy's Seafood, New York, NY
                    Cook, Summer 1988
                    Prepared and cooked assorted seafood dishes. Accounted
                    for deliveries and receiving.

                    Jones Construction, Brooklyn, NY
                    General Laborer and Driver, Summer 1986-87
                    Operated heavy machinery and handled other aspects
                    of my job including delivering materials to and from
                    various job sites.

ACTIVITIES AND
HONORS: Beta Alpha Psi (Communications Honor Society), 1990
                    Dean's List, Fall 1988 & Spring 1990
                    A.I.S.E.C. - Association for International Business
                    Played on racquetball and tennis teams

REFERENCES: Available upon request

PEDRO C. GONZALES
7 E. Pullman Road
Chicago, IL 60634
312/555-4560

OBJECTIVE: A position as a sales representative in which I
employ my sales and communications skills.

WORK
EXPERIENCE: Belwin-Mills Inc., Chicago, IL
Salesman, 1987 - 1990
Sold sheet music to retail businesses. Named top
salesman of 1986. Maintained good customer
relations by identifying customer needs. Trained
new sales representatives and advised them on
effective selling techniques.

Fuller Brush Co., Aurora, IL
Salesman, 1982 - 1987
Sold products for the home in the South suburban
Chicago area. Increased territory sales by 85% in
five years. Demonstrated and planned specific
uses for products in the household. Maintained
constant contact with accounts.

EDUCATION: Fuller Brush Training Course, Aurora, IL
Summer 1982

Barton Technical High School, Chicago, IL
Graduated 1981
Tennis Team, Co-captain

REFERENCES: Available upon request

RUTH M. DAVID

572 FIRST STREET
BROOKLYN, NY 11215
(212) 555-4328

Education

Princeton University, Princeton, NJ
Degree expected: MBA, June 1990
Class Rank: Top Twenty-five Percent

Honors: Associate Editor, Business Journal

University of Wisconsin, Madison, WI
B.A. in Political Science, May 1988

Honors: Dean's List
         Marching Band Drill Instructor, Section Leader
         Residence Hall Council President

Business
Experience

International Business Machines, White Plains, NY
Intern/Sales, 6/89 - 9/89
Assisted in PC Sales Division. Worked to promote
distribution to retail outlets. Helped to coordinate
product demonstration program used throughout the
country.

Other Experience

Citizen Action Group, New York, NY
Field Manager, 6/88 - 9/88
Promoted citizen awareness of state legislative process
and issues of toxic waste, utility control and consumer
legislation. Demonstrated effective fund raising and
communication methods to the canvass employees. Developed
and sustained employee motivation and productivity.

University of Wisconsin, Madison, WI
Resident Assistant, Office of Residential Life, 8/86 - 5/88
Administered all aspects of student affairs in university
residence halls, including program planning, discipline
and individual group counseling. Directed achievement of
student goals through guidance of the residence hall
council. Developed and implemented university policies.

University of Wisconsin, Madison, WI
Staff Training Lecturer, 8/87 - 11/88
Conducted workshops for residence hall staff on counseling
and effective communication.

References

Available on request

THOMAS FORESTER
Fulton Hall
2300 East Harrison
Room 306
Chicago, IL 60633
312/555-4849

OBJECTIVE: A career in sales and marketing.

EDUCATION: University of Illinois at Chicago, Chicago,
                   IL
                   Bachelor of Arts in Economics
                   Expected June 1991

HONORS: Phi Beta Kappa
                   Dean's list five times
                   Robeson Economics Scholarship, 1989

ACTIVITIES: Vice President, Beta Gamma Fraternity
                   Freshman Advisor
                   Homecoming Planning Committee
                   Baseball Team
                   Student Rights Group

WORK
EXPERIENCE: IBM, Northbrook, IL
                   Marketing Intern, 1990
                   Assisted marketing staff in the areas of
                   research, demographics, sales forecasts,
                   identifying new customers and promotion.

                   University of Illinois at Chicago
                   Office Assistant, Journalism School, 1988-
                   1990
                   Assisted with registrations, filing and
                   typing. Arranged application materials.
                   Assembled course packs.

                   General Office, Registrar, 1988
                   Processed transcript requests. Entered
                   registrations on the computer. Provided
                   informational assistance to students.

SPECIAL SKILLS: Hands-on computer experience using LOTUS 123
                   and dBASE III.

REFERENCES: Available on request.

RENEE GYLKISON
8 E. Western Avenue
Houston, TX 75737
713/555-8098

JOB OBJECTIVE

A position as assistant manager of publishing company.

ACHIEVEMENTS

* Orchestrated market analyses and researched competition for reports to the
  district manager.
* Identified clients' needs and problems and assured them of personal
  attention.
* Prepared sales forecasts and sales goals reports.
* Resolved service and billing problems.
* Developed monthly sales plans which identified necessary account maintenance
  and specific problems that required attention.
* Delivered sales presentations to groups and individuals.
* Maintained daily sales logs and referral logs.
* Identified potential new clients and established new accounts.
* Increased client base by 50%.

EMPLOYMENT HISTORY

American National Inc., Houston, TX
Sales Representative, 1988 - present

Unico International, Dallas, TX
Sales Representative, 1985 - 1988

Red's Shoes, Omaha, NE
Salesperson, 1984 - 1985

Tex Mex Tacos, Austin, TX
Management Trainee, 1984

EDUCATION

Austin College, Austin, TX
B.A. in History, 1984

REFERENCES

Provided upon request

CHRISTOPHER POLLEN
8909 S. Alvira St.
Los Angeles, CA 90028
000/989-9090

OBJECTIVE

To obtain a position in market research where I can focus on needs/trends analysis, demographics and market surveys.

WORK EXPERIENCE

SOUTHERN CALIFORNIA TOURS, INC., Los Angeles, CA
RESEARCH ANALYST ASSISTANT, 1987 to present
Projected sales potential by interpreting sales figures from yearly data; developed a target program that increased the efficiency of company's direct mail campaign; analyzed incoming market data on customers for demographic purposes; initiated changes in marketing strategy which improved customer satisfaction.

AMERICAN HOSPITAL SUPPLY CORP., Evanston, IL
SALES ASSISTANT, 1983-1986
Researched and wrote training bulletins on communication and sales strategy for the sales staff; trained new sales people; prepared proposals for the regional sales manager; handled scheduling and travel arrangements for the sales department.

EDUCATION

NORTHWESTERN UNIVERSITY, Evanston, IL
B.A. in English, 1983

HONORS

Graduated with honors in English, 1983
Dean's List, 1982, 1983

ACTIVITIES

President, Senior Writing Club, 1983
Captain, Men's Tennis Team, 1982-1983

SPECIAL SKILLS

Hands-on computer experience using Lotus 1-2-3 and Wordstar.
Working knowledge of French and German.

References available upon request

JASMINE TOPPER
5 E. Randall Road
Providence, RI 00898
401/555-6768

OBJECTIVE: Assistant sales manager.

WORK
HISTORY: American Telecom, Providence, RI
               Sales Representative, 1988 - present
               Identified customers' needs and problems and assured them of
               personal attention. Delivered sales presentations to groups
               and individuals. Identified potential new customers and
               established new accounts. Increased client base by 30%.
               Prepared sales forecasts and sales reports.

               Amandala Foods, Inc., Boston, MA
               Sales Representative, 1985 - 1988
               Orchestrated market analyses and researched competition for
               reports to the district manager. Developed monthly sales
               plans which identified necessary account maintenance and
               specific problems that required attention. Resolved service
               and billing problems. Maintained daily sales logs and referral
               logs.

               Century 21 Realty, Cambridge, MA
               Salesperson, 1971 - 1981
               Sold homes in the Cambridge area. Interacted with clients,
               real estate agents, brokers and bank personnel. Awarded
               salesperson of the year three times.

EDUCATION: Cambridge College, Cambridge, MA
               B.A. in Business, 1985
               Received Harriet Johnson Business Scholarship

               Boston Community College, Boston, MA
               1970 - 1971

SPECIAL
SKILLS: Proficient on Word Perfect 5 and Lotus 123.

               References available

GINA STEVENSON
433 Maple Drive
Hoffman Estates, IL 60035
708/555-2341

OBJECTIVE

To become a part of the sales and marketing team at Laura Ashley, Inc.

WORK EXPERIENCE

Gina Designs, Hoffman Estates, IL
Owner/Designer, 1980 - present
Established a national market for my original clothing line. Displayed
and merchandised clothing items at retail stores and fashion shows.
Increased sales 300% in the past two years. Ordered supplies, processed
purchase orders and invoices. Shipped and delivered products.

Talbot's Inc., Schaumburg, IL
Assistant Sales Manager, 1981 - present
Sold clothing and gifts at the retail level. Increased sales by developing
in-store sales promotions. Ordered stock and maintained inventory.

Lynn's Hallmark, Arlington Heights, IL
Sales Person, 1970 - 1974
Manager, 1975-1980
Managed gift shop and supervised 10 employees. Maintained inventory, sales
records and bank deposits. Ordered products, processed purchase orders and
invoices. Handled all payroll duties. Sold gift items.

EDUCATION

B.A., Interior Design, Wheaton College, Wheaton, IL, 1980

SPECIAL SKILLS

Working knowledge of Spanish.
Experience working with WORD PERFECT V & DISPLAYWRITE IV.

REFERENCES

Provided on request

QUENTIN PORLEAN
12½ Derbyshire Dr.
East St. Louis, IL 60989
314/555-8932

JOB SOUGHT

A position as manager of an electronics department of a major department store.

WORK EXPERIENCE

Bergstrom's, St. Louis, MO

Assistant Manager, 1989 - present
Salesperson, 1987 - 1989
Customer Service Representative, 1986 - 1987
Promoted from customer service representative to salesperson and then to assistant manager of electronics at Bergstrom's. Managed a staff of four, including hiring, job training and supervision. Helped to reorganize inventory control methods. Assisted customers in choosing electronic products and designing entertainment centers. Combined managerial and sales talents which increased sales.

Radio Shack, East St. Louis, IL
Salesperson, Summers 1984 - 1986
Sold electronic products and equipment. Handled inventory and product orders. Assisted customers with technical questions.

EDUCATION

East St. Louis High School, East St. Louis, IL
Graduated June 1986
Top 15% of class
Student Council President
Black Students Alliance

Barton Community College, St. Louis, MO
Attended 1989
Courses included "Sales Techinques" and "Retail Management"

St. Louis Chamber of Commerce Retail Convention, 1989

REFERENCES

Provided on request

JOANNA P. DOBSON

5660 W. 7th St.   (600) 455-3453 (Day)
Des Moines, IA 50399   (600) 359-9000 (Evening)

OBJECTIVE

To be placed in a marketing research position where I can assist in the
development of marketing and sales strategies for a major medical supplies
company.

ACHIEVEMENTS

Developed and implemented marketing strategies for a major manufacturer of
of disposable medical supplies sold for the purposes of anesthesia
administration, IV therapy and open-heart surgery.

Served as a research and development specialist for a surgical supply
manufacturer.

Managed a five state sales area on the east coast. Increased sales 38%
during my three year tenure as a surgical supplies sales representative.
Increased number of clients by 27% which led to a significant increase
in revenue.

WORK EXPERIENCE

Amicon, Inc, Des Moines, IA
Marketing Assistant, 1987 to present

Meico Surgical Co., Carbondale, IL
Research and Development Assistant, 1985-1987

US Medical, Harrisburg, PA
Sales Representative, 1983-1987

EDUCATION

B.S., Biology, University of Pennsylvania, 1982
Graduated in top 10% of class.

REFERENCES

Available upon request

SHAWANA HODGES
5678 N. Riverside Dr.
Burbank, CA 91505
818/555-8989
818/555-1000

CAREER OBJECTIVE: Sales representative for an office supplies company.

ACHIEVEMENTS: *Handled price quotations, information on product line,
                      customer inquiries on shipments and special orders.

                     *Assisted sales manager in various office activities and
                      procedures.

                     *Arranged travel and transportation, hotel and scheduling
                      of seminars and meetings.

                     *Drafted monthly reports on sales procedures and profit
                      margins.

                     *Managed computerization of office records.

                     *Routed editing duties and proofreading responsibilities.

                     *Edited and proofread inter-office memos and a weekly
                      department newsletter.

                     *Supervised two student interns.

EMPLOYMENT
HISTORY: Sanco Office Supplies Ltd., Burbank, CA
                     Executive Secretary to Sales Manager, 1985 - present

                     Popular Artists Management, Los Angeles, CA
                     Secretary to Manager of Publications, 1983 - 1985

EDUCATION: Pasadena College, Pasadena, CA
                     B.S. in Marketing, 1987
                     Evening Division

                     Commercial School of Business, Los Angeles, CA
                     Completed advanced secretarial course

SPECIAL SKILLS: Proficiency on IBM and DATATECH hardware and WORDSTAR,
                     SOFTMATE and MULTIMATE software.

                     References available.

JOHNNY KAZELL
5320 Wilshire Blvd.
Los Angeles, CA   90069
213/555-9282

OBJECTIVE: Seeking a marketing position in the music industry.

WORK
EXPERIENCE: WRT Records, Los Angeles, CA
Marketing Director, 9/88 - present
Handled distribution, retail marketing, advertising and
mail order marketing. Wrote biographies and coordinated
publicity. Obtained knowledge regarding domestic and
overseas independent distribution, buyers for U.S. chain
stores and Billboard reporters.

Hit Productions, Los Angeles, CA
Public Relations/Marketing Assistant, 5/87 - 9/88
Assisted PR Director with all duties, including radio
promotion and retail marketing. Coordinated radio and
print interviews for artists. Typing, filing and answering
phones.

KTWV Radio, Los Angeles, CA
Music Director, 6/86 - 5/87
Selected appropriate music for a contemporary jazz format.
Oversaw daily operations of music library and programming
department. Supervised a staff of six.

EDUCATION: UCLA, Los Angeles, CA
B.A. in Arts Management, May 1985

ACTIVITIES: Phi Mu Alpha Music Fraternity, President
National Association of College Activities
Alpha Lambda Fraternity

SPECIAL
SKILLS: Working knowledge of Microsoft Word and Lotus 123.

References available on request.

JAMES KENDALL

Address: 509 27th St., #4556
                    New York, NY 10019

Phone: 212/555-9809
                    212/555-7777

Professional
Experience: Jones and Jones, New York, NY
                    Commodity Broker, 1988 - present
                    Handled over 500 clients as a specialist in corn
                    and wheat futures. Provided written market forecasts
                    to sales people. Published and distributed a weekly
                    newsletter on futures.

                    Karen Schwartz, Inc., New York, NY
                    Commodity Sales, 1980-1987
                    Managed a client list of over 300. Researched and wrote
                    in-house reports on wheat market forecasts. Named
                    salesperson of the year, 1985.

                    Pickering, Pickering & Gold, Chicago, IL
                    Commodity trader, 1975-1980
                    Traded cattle futures in-pit on the Chicago Commodities
                    Exchange.

Education: B.A., Brown University, 1975.
                    Major: Economics
                    Minor: English

Professional
Memberships: American Society of Commodities Brokers

Seminars: "Commodity Futures"
                    University of Wisconsin, Madison, 1984

Special
Abilities: Will relocate.

References: Available on request

JIM HORNFELD
1800 W. Third St.
Apartment 1001
San Francisco, CA   98088
415/555-9202

OBJECTIVE: A management position in sales and marketing.

PROFESSIONAL
EXPERIENCE: Rolex Watches, Inc., San Francisco, CA
                  Vice President of Sales and Marketing, 1979 - present
                  Increased watch sales from $3 million to $12 million during
                  the past six years. Introduced new and existing product lines
                  through presentations to marketing directors and manufacturers.
                  Developed fifteen new accounts. Supervised five sales agencies
                  throughout the U.S. and Canada. Developed new products expanding
                  from watches to other accessories which resulted in increased sales.
                  Researched watch market in order to coordinate product line with
                  current fashion trends. Increased company's share of the market
                  through improved quality products.

                  Peters and Company, Salt Lake City, UT
                  District Sales Manager, 1974 - 1979
                  Planned successful strategies to identify and develop new
                  accounts. Increased sales by at least 25% each year.
                  Researched and analyzed market conditions in order to seek out
                  new customers. Developed weekly and monthly sales strategies.
                  Supervised seven sales representatives.

                  Herzz, Inc., Los Angeles, CA
                  Sales Representative, 1969 - 1974
                  Developed and managed new territories. Built sales through
                  calls on retailers and wholesalers. Developed creative
                  techniques for increasing product sales. Maintained current
                  knowledge of competitive products. Wrote weekly and monthly
                  sales reports.

EDUCATION: University of Southern California, Los Angeles, CA
                  B.S. in Marketing, 1968

SEMINARS: Southern California Marketing Seminar, 1987 - 1990
                  National Retailers Association, 1982 - 1986

REFERENCES: Available on request

MARION ZARET
3333 W. 57th St.
Apartment 12E
Brooklyn, NY 12909
718/555-2323
718/555-4999

OBJECTIVE: Public relations director for Soft Drink Company.

WORK
EXPERIENCE: <u>Coca Cola, Inc.</u>, New York, NY
                 National Sales Manager, 1987 - present
                 Account Manager, 1985 - 1987
                 Assistant Account Manager, 1984 - 1985
                 Personnel Assistant, 1982 - 1984
                 Receptionist, 1980 - 1982

                 Managed a sales/marketing staff which included account managers
                 and sales representatives. Monitored and studed the effectiveness
                 of a national distribution network. Represented company to
                 clients and retailers in order to present new products. Organized
                 and planned convention displays and strategy. Oversaw all aspects
                 of sales/marketing budget. Designed and executed direct mail
                 program that identified marketplace needs and new options for
                 products. Conceived ads, posters and point-of-purchase materials
                 for products. Initiated and published a monthly newsletter that
                 was distributed to current and potential customers.

EDUCATION: <u>American University</u>, White Plains, NY
                 B.A. in English, 1979

SEMINARS: American Marketing Association Seminars, 1985 - 1990
                 Coca Cola Internal Sales Workshops, 1986 - 1990
                 Soft Drink Industry Conventions

SPECIAL
SKILLS: Computer literate in FORTRAN and BASIC. Experience using
                 SOFTMATE and MULTIMATE software.

                 References available on request

Christopher Knight
1700 W. Armadillo
San Diego, CA 90087
619/555-9000
619/555-2839

OBJECTIVE: To obtain a position as Vice President of Sales in a major
aeronautical corporation.

AREAS OF EXPERIENCE:

Marketing Development

>   *Initiated and supervised sales programs for aircraft
>   distributers selling aircraft to businesses throughout the
>   western United States.
>
>   *Managed accounts with a profit range of $100,000 to $1,000,000,
>   including Dow Chemical, Landston Steel, Mercury Co., Berkeley
>   Metallurgical & Ford Motor Co.
>
>   *Demonstrated to customer companies how to use aircraft to
>   coordinate and consolidate expanding facilities.
>
>   *Introduced and expanded use of aircraft for musical tours.

Public Relations

>   *Handled all levels of sales promotion, corporate public relations and
>   training of industry on company use of aircraft.
>
>   *Managed promotions including personal presentations, radio & TV
>   broadcasts, news stories and magazine features.

Pilot Training

>   *Taught primary, secondary and instrument flight in single and
>   multi-engine aircraft.

Christopher Knight - 2

EMPLOYMENT HISTORY: Hughes Aircraft, Inc., San Diego, CA
Sales Manager and Chief Pilot, 1981 - present

Boeing Corporation, Kansas City, MO
Assistant Manager of Promotion, 1972 - 1980

American Airlines, Dallas, TX
Pilot, 1965 - 1972

United States Airforce, Houston, TX
Flight Instructor, 1963 - 1965

PROFESSIONAL
LICENSE: Airline Transport Rating 14352-60
Single, Multi-Engine-Land
Flight Instructor - Instrument

EDUCATION: University of Texas, Houston, TX
B.A. in History, 1961

MILITARY
SERVICE: United States Air Force
1963 - 1965

REFERENCES: Available on request

CAROLINE A. CAROLSON
5001 Irvine Meadows Drive
Calistoga, FL 28088
305/555-8398

OBJECTIVE: A management level sales position.

EMPLOYMENT
HISTORY: **Simpco, Inc.**, Tampa, FL
                  Regional Sales Manager, 1983 - present
                  Managed sales of all product lines in southern
                  markets for a leading manufacturer of fixtures.
                  Represented five corporate divisions of the
                  company with sales in excess of $2 million
                  annually. Directed and motivated a sales force of
                  12 in planned selling to achieve company goals.

                  Lucky Industries, Miami, FL
                  District Manager, 1978 - 1983
                  Acted as sales representative for the Miami
                  metropolitan area. Built both wholesale and
                  dealer distribution substantially during my
                  tenure. Developed monthly sales plans which
                  identified necessary account maintenance and
                  specific problems that required attention.

                  National Office Products, Inc., Baton Rouge, LA
                  Assistant Sales Manager, 1969 - 1978
                  Handled both internal and external areas of sales
                  and marketing, including samples, advertising and
                  pricing. Served as company sales representative
                  and sold a variety of office supplies to retail
                  stores.

EDUCATION: **Smith College**, Omaha, NE
                  B.A. in English, 1967

SEMINARS: American Sales Association Seminars, 1985 - 1990

REFERENCES: Available on request.

SARA STEVENS

332 E. Geobert Rd.
Terre Haute, IN 48930
317/555-3890

JOB OBJECTIVE: Manager of a florist shop.

WORK
EXPERIENCE: TERRY'S FLOWERS, Terre Haute, IN
                    Assistant Sales Manager, 1989 - present

                    Sold flowers, waited on customers, filled phone orders,
                    handled special orders and designed window displays.
                    Handled the placing of ads for a major advertising
                    campaign. Represented store at conventions.

                    AVANT BOOKS, Indianapolis, IN

                    Sold books to customers, filled special orders and
                    arranged inventory. Handled customer returns and
                    special requests.

EDUCATION: REVERS HIGH SCHOOL, Indianapolis, IN

                    Graduated June 1988
                    Ranked 15 in a class of 250
                    Worked in student bookstore for four years.

REFERENCES: Available on request

SIDNEY HARRIS, JR.
234 E. Norway St.   #4
Boston, MA   12889
602/555-1828
602/555-2020

OBJECTIVE: The position of senior vice president of sales and
                    marketing at Potter Foods, Inc.

PROFESSIONAL
ACHIEVEMENTS: <u>Sales</u>

                    * Introduced new and existing product lines
                    through presentations to major clients.
                    * Increased sales from $27 million to $50 million
                      in five years.
                    * Initiated and developed nine new accounts.
                    * Supervised five sales agencies throughout the
                      U.S.

                    <u>Marketing</u>

                    * Researched computer market in order to
                    coordinate product line with current public tastes
                    and buying trends.
                    * Developed new approaches to marketing food
                    products, including in-store displays and
                    advertising.
                    * Organized and planned convention displays and
                      strategies.

EMPLOYMENT
HISTORY: <u>Potter Foods, Inc.</u>, Boston, MA
                    Sales and Marketing Manager, 1985 - present

                    <u>Westco</u>, Providence, RI
                    Product Coordinator, 1980 - 1985

                    <u>Go-West, Inc.</u>, Canoga Falls, NY
                    Sales Representative, 1975 - 1980

EDUCATION: <u>Boston University</u>, Boston, MA
                    B.S. 1975
                    Major: Business Administration
                    Minor: Computer Science

REFERENCES: Available upon request

GRISSETE ALEMANN

1202 W. North Ave.   312/555-8908
Chicago, IL   60645   312/555-7200

OBJECTIVE: A position in sales management.

**WORK
EXPERIENCE:**   <u>Gandy's Shoes</u>, Chicago, IL
Assistant Manager, 1987 - present
Served as assistant manager of a quality shoe
store with partial supervision of seven
salespeople. Researched customer's buying habits
and preferences. Handled promotion and mailings
for special sales and in-store events. Helped to
increase sales through personal attention to
customer needs.

<u>Flaherty Jewelers</u>, Arlington Heights, IL
Salesperson, 1980 - 1987
Sold jewelry at a fine jewelry store. Greeted
customers and advised them on their needs.
Generated repeat business by encouraging customers
to return. Entered data on computer to keep track
of inventory. Handled returns and orders from
distributor. Designed displays for store.

<u>Canon Co.</u>, Atlanta, GA
Sales representative, 1975 -1980
Sold and serviced office copiers to businesses and
schools in the greater Atlanta area. Maintained
good customer relations through frequent calls and
visits. Identified potential customers.

EDUCATION: <u>Atlanta Community College</u>, Atlanta, GA
Attended two years. Majored in Business.

<u>Central High School</u>, Marietta, GA
Graduated 1980. Won Math award.

REFERENCES: Available on request.

SERITA TERESA WOODMAN
4553 N. Alamo Avenue
Dallas, TX 74667
216/555-8908

OBJECTIVE: Sales manager for a company that markets vacation packages.

EXPERIENCE: American Airlines, Inc., Dallas, TX
Sales representative, 1988 - present
Sold reservations for domestic flights, hotels and car rentals. Marketed travel packages through travel agencies. Negotiated airline and hotel discounts for customers. Devised itineraries and solved customers' travel related problems.

Salt Lake Travel, Salt Lake City, UT
Travel Agent, 1980 - 1988
Handled customer reservations for airlines, hotels, and car rentals. Advised customers on competitive travel packages and prices. Interacted with all major airlines, hotel chains and car rental companies.

EDUCATION: University of Illinois, Urbana, IL
B.A. in Anthropology, 1956

SPECIAL
SKILLS: Hands-on experience using most travel-related computer systems, including Apollo.

Working knowledge of German, French and Polish.

REFERENCES: Available on request.

```
HAROLD C. JONES
Bobb Hall
6 W. Allis Drive
Room 34
Pittsburgh, PA  28920
404/555-2384
```

OBJECTIVE: Position in the field of sales.

EDUCATION: <u>University of Pittsburgh</u>, Pittsburgh, PA
                        Bachelor of Arts in Economics
                        Expected June 1991

HONORS: Pitt Honorary Scholar
                        Pennsylvania Honor Society
                        Freshman Economics Scholarship, 1989

ACTIVITIES: Student Government
                        Freshman Advisor
                        Homecoming Planning Committee
                        Basketball Team

WORK
EXPERIENCE: <u>Nabisco, Inc.</u>, Philadelphia, PA
                        Sales Intern, 1990
                        Assisted sales staff in the areas of
                        research, demographics, sales forecasts,
                        identifying new customers and promotion.

                        <u>University of Pittsburgh</u>, Pittsburgh, PA
                        General Office, Registrar, 1988
                        Processed transcript requests. Entered
                        registrations on the computer. Provided
                        informational assistance to students.

SPECIAL SKILLS: Able to translate Spanish. Experience using
                        LOTUS 123 and dBASE III software programs.

REFERENCES: Available on request.

IVAR T. KOPESKI

501 W. GLENDALE BLVD.
KANSAS CITY, MO 51132
816/555-3524
816/555-9090

OBJECTIVE

Regional sales manager for a national manufacturer/distributor

EXPERIENCE

REB Pharmaceuticals, Kansas City, MO
District Sales Manager, 1984 - 1990
Directed the selling and servicing of accounts to physicians, pharmacies
and hospitals in the Kansas City area. Increased sales by 50% in three
years. Initiated an incentive plan which resulted in 21 new accounts.
Worked with production department to improve product quality.

Jacobs & Jacobs Advertising, Trenton, NJ
Display Coordinator, 1981 - 1984
Coordinated and supervised the installation of displays in men's clothing
stores in the Trenton area. Managed a five-person office in all aspects
of display planning and production. Worked to help place the firm in the
syndicated display advertising field.

Mark Shale, Inc., Schaumburg, IL
Retail Store Manager, 1977 - 1981
Promoted from salesperson to assistant manager to manager within two years.
Supervised the designing of display for interior and windows. Handled all
aspects of personnel, sales promotions, inventory control and new product.
Interacted with corporate management frequently.

EDUCATION

Harper College, Palatine, IL
Attended two years (1975 - 1977) and majored in advertising.

American Institute, Putnum, NJ
Completed course on Sales and Marketing Techniques, 1983

MEMBERSHIPS

American Display Advertisers
Kansas City Sales Association
Kansas City Community Development Association

REFERENCES

Available on request

CLARENCE SCOTT TALLEY III
600 W. Porter St.
5
Las Vegas, NV 89890
514/555-3893

EDUCATION

<u>University of Nevada</u>, Las Vegas, NV
Bachelor of Science in Marketing
Expected June 1991

HONORS

Dean's List four semesters
Dornburn Scholarship
UNLV Marketing Award

ACTIVITIES

President, Kappa Beta Fraternity
New Student Week Committee
Homecoming Planning Committee
Captain, Tennis Team

WORK EXPERIENCE

<u>Porter Rand & Associates</u>, Seattle, WA
Marketing Intern, 1990
Assisted sales staff in the areas of research,
demographics, sales forecasts, identifying new
customers and promotion.

<u>University of Nevada</u>, Las Vegas, NV
Research/Office Assistant, 1988-89
Researched and compiled materials for department
professors. Arranged filing system and supervisor's
library. Organized department inventory.

SPECIAL SKILLS

Experience using IBM and APPLE hardware and WORDSTAR
and dBASE III software programs.

References available

SARA WOODS
4400 Sunset Blvd.
Los Angeles, CA 90028
213/555-8989
213/555-6666

OBJECTIVE: A position in sales management.

ACHIEVEMENTS: * Planned successful strategies to identify and develop new accounts.
               * Increased sales by at least 20% each year as District Sales
                 Manager.
               * Researched and analyzed market conditions in order to seek out
                 new customers.
               * Developed weekly and monthly sales strategies.
               * Supervised seven sales representatives.
               * Conducted field visits to solve customer complaints.
               * Maintained daily customer contact to insure good customer/
                 company relations.
               * Wrote product information fliers and distributed them through
                 a direct mail program.

WORK
EXPERIENCE: Southern California Fruit Co., Los Angeles, CA
               District Sales Manager, 1986 - present

               L.A. Freight Co., Los Angeles, CA
               Account Executive, 1984 - 1986

               Handlemen & Associates, Santa Rita, CA
               Sales Representative, 1983 - 1984

EDUCATION: University of Colorado, Boulder, CO
               B.A., 1983
               Major: Management
               Minor: Political Science
               G.P.A. 3.3/4.0

PROFESSIONAL
MEMBERSHIPS: Southern California Sales Association, Treasurer, 1988 - 1990
               Los Angeles Chamber of Commerce, 1986 - present

SPECIAL
SKILLS: DOS experience. LOTUS/DBASE/WORD PERFECT experience.

REFERENCES: Provided on request

DENNISE LAY
706 E. 76th St. #445
Ft. Lauderdale, FL 28088
305/555-3434

OBJECTIVE: A sales position at the management level.

EMPLOYMENT
HISTORY: **Yolanda Cosmetics, Inc.**, Miami, FL
                  Regional Sales Manager, 1983 - present
                  Managed sales of all product lines in southern
                  markets for a leading manufacturer of cosmetics.
                  Represented five corporate divisions of the
                  company with sales in excess of $2 million
                  annually. Directed and motivated a sales force of
                  12 in planned selling to achieve company goals.

                  Collins Video Corp., Miami, FL
                  District Manager, 1978 - 1983
                  Acted as sales representative for the Miami
                  metropolitan area. Built both wholesale and
                  dealer distribution substantially during my
                  tenure. Developed monthly sales plans which
                  identified necessary account maintenance and
                  specific problems that required attention.

                  American Office Products, Inc., Biloxi, MS
                  Assistant Sales Manager, 1969 - 1978
                  Handled both internal and external areas of sales
                  and marketing, including samples, advertising and
                  pricing. Served as company sales representative
                  and sold a variety of office supplies to retail
                  stores.

EDUCATION: **Smith College**, Kansas City, MO
                  B.A. in English, 1967

SEMINARS: American Sales Association Seminars, 1985 - 1990

REFERENCES: Available on request.

DAVID P. JENKINS
3663 N. Coldwater Canyon
North Hollywood, CA 90390
818/555-3472
818/555-3678

JOB OBJECTIVE: A position as a sales/marketing manager where I can ultilize
                 my knowledge and experience by combining high volume selling
                 of major accounts with an administrative ability that increases
                 sales through encouragement of sales team.

EMPLOYMENT
HISTORY: Tribor Industries, Los Angeles, CA
                 Regional Sales Manager, 1985 - present
                 Managed sales of all product lines in western markets for a
                 leading maker of linens. Represented five corporate divisions
                 of the company with sales in excess of $3,000,000 annually.
                 Directed and motivated a sales force of 12 sales representatives
                 in planned selling to achieve company goals.

                 Tribor Industries, Los Angeles, CA
                 District Manager, 1980 - 1985
                 Acted as sales representive for the Los Angeles metropolitan
                 area. Built both wholesale and dealer distribution substantially
                 during my tenure. Promoted to Regional Sales Manager after five
                 years service.

                 American Office Supply, Chicago, IL
                 Assisant to Sales Manager, 1976 - 1980
                 Handled both internal and external areas of sales and marketing,
                 including samples, advertising and pricing. Served as company
                 sales representative and sold a variety of office supplies to
                 retail stores.

EDUCATION: University of Michigan, Ann Arbor, MI
                 B.A. Business Administration, 1975
                 Major Field: Management

SEMINARS: National Management Association Seminar, 1984
                 Purdue University Seminars, 1987, 1988

PROFESSIONAL
MEMBERSHIPS: Sales and Marketing Association of Los Angeles
                 National Association of Market Developers

REFERENCES: Available upon request

RANDALL COURY

62 Collins Place
#43
New Orleans, LA 33290
504/555-3490
504/555-3999

OBJECTIVE

A position as manager of a record store.

EMPLOYMENT HISTORY

WEST RECORDS, New Orleans, LA
Assistant Manager, 1989 - present

Sold records, waited on customers, assisted in product selection
and ordering, handled special orders and returned merchandise.
Designed window displays. Oversaw the placement of ads for a
major advertising campaign. Represented store at conventions.

THE BELT STORE, West Lake, LA
Salesperson, 1987 - 1988

Sold accesories to customers, filled special orders, organized
and arranged inventory. Handled customer returns and special
requests. Assisted in the design of window displays.

EDUCATION

EAST CENTRAL HIGH SCHOOL, New Orleans, LA

Graduated June 1988
Ranked 12 in a class of 200
Tennis Team
Homecoming Committee

REFERENCES

Available on request

ALLISON SPRINGS
15 Hilton House
College de l'Art Libre
Smallville, CO 77717
303/555-2550

Job Sought: Food Industry Sales Representative

Skills and Experience

Negotiating Skills: Developed negotiating skills through participation in
                       student government which enabled me both to persuade
                       others of the advatages to them of a contrary position
                       and to reach a compromise between people who wish to
                       pursue different goals.

Promotional Skills: Contributed greatly to my successful campaign for class
                       office (Junior Class Vice President) through the effective
                       use of posters, displays and other visual aids. Participated
                       in committee projects and fund raising efforts which netted
                       $15,000 for the junior class project.

People Skills: As Junior Class Vice President, balanced the concerns of
                       different groups in order to reach a common goal. As
                       a claims interviewer with a state public assistance agency,
                       dealt with people under stressful circumstances. As a
                       research assistant with a law firm, interacted both with
                       lawyers and clerical workers. As a lifeguard, learned how
                       to manage groups.

Education   College de l'Art Libre, Smallville, CO
                        Bachelor of Arts in Political Science
                        Degree expected June 1991
                        Vice President Junior Class
                        Student Council
                        Harvest Committee

Work Experience   McCall, McCrow & McCoy, Westrow, CO
                        Research Assistant, January 1990 to present

                        Department of Public Assistance, Smallville, CO
                        Claims Interviewer, September 1989 - December 1989

                        Shilo Pool, Shilo, NE
                        Lifeguard, 1985 - 1988

References   Provided on request

DIANA SIMPLETON
2323 Canon Drive
Beverly Hills, CA 90120
Telephone: 213/555-8920

OBJECTIVE

An entry-level position in a market research firm with an opportunity to
advance to management level.

ACHIEVEMENTS

Sales/Promotion

*Sold Elizabeth Arden cosmetic products in two major retail stores.

*Orchestrated product demonstrations to customers in-store.

*Designed displays of merchandise.

*Represented Elizabeth Arden at promotional events in the Los Angeles area
 advising customers on the use of skin care products.

*Maintained inventory and handled monthly sales reports.

*Developed an advertising campaign for a line of women's clothing as a
 class assignment that addressed distribution, market share and sales promotion.

Management

*Managed Elizabeth Arden counter at The Broadway and at May's.

*Supervised three salespeople.

*Gained knowledge of marketing management techniques through classes.

EMPLOYMENT HISTORY

Elizabeth Arden, The Broadway, Glendale, CA
Counter Manager, 1987 - present

Elizabeth Arden, May's Department Store, Beverly Hills, CA
Retail Salesperson, 1985 - 1987

Geffen Records, Los Angeles, CA
Switchboard Operator, 1984

EDUCATION

B.S. in Business from Santa Clara College, Santa Clara, CA - 1984

REFERENCES PROVIDED ON REQUEST

EUGENE T. SHOW

432 Sentinel Ave.
Kansas City, MO 74309
816/555-3903

OBJECTIVE: A career in sales/marketing.

EDUCATION: STEVENS COLLEGE, Kansas City, MO

                   B.A. in Marketing, 1990
                   Honor Society
                   3.66 GPA in major field
                   3.44 GPA overall
                   Student Government Secretary
                   Homecoming Committee

                   Plan to pursue a Master's degree at a future date.

                   EASTERN CITY HIGH SCHOOL, Portland, OR

                   Graduated 1986
                   Salutatorian
                   President of Senior Class
                   Drama Club
                   Soccer Team

WORK
EXPERIENCE: ANDERS ADVERTISING, INC., Kansas City, MO
                   Marketing Intern, Summer 1989
                   Assisted Marketing Manager in areas of promotion, product
                   development and demographic analysis.

                   SURVEY SERVICE, INC., Kansas City, MO
                   Telephone Surveyor, Summer 1987 & 1988

                   RADICAL RECORDS, East Lydon, MO
                   Salesperson, Summer 1986

SPECIAL
SKILLS: Working knowledge of German, French and Spanish. Familiarity
                   with several computer software programs.

                   References available

LUIS SANCHEZ

4742 N. Lawndale
Chicago, IL 60625
312/555-2574

OBJECTIVE: Sales manager of Good's Video Store.

WORK
EXPERIENCE: <u>Good's Video</u>, Chicago, IL
                Assistant Manager, 1987 - present
                Served as assistant manager of a full-service
                video store with partial supervision of seven
                salespeople. Researched customer's buying habits
                and preferences. Handled promotion and mailings
                for special sales and in-store events. Helped to
                increase sales through personal attention to
                customer needs.

                <u>Johnson Florists</u>, Chicago, IL
                Salesperson, 1980 - 1987
                Sold flowers. Greeted customers and advised them
                on their needs. Generated repeat business by
                encouraging customers to return. Entered data on
                computer to keep track of inventory. Handled
                returns and orders form distributor. Designed
                displays for store.

                <u>Mita Co.</u>, Chicago, IL
                Sales representative, 1975 -1980
                Sold and serviced office copiers to businesses and
                schools in the greater Chicago area. Maintained
                good customer relations through frequent calls and
                visits. Identified potential customers.

EDUCATION: <u>Northeastern Illinois University</u>, Chicago, IL
                Attended two years. Majored in Business.

                <u>Central High School</u>, Chicago, IL
                Graduated 1980. Won Math award.

REFERENCES: Available on request.

REBECCA ROBINSON
1801 Kirchoff Rd.
Rolling Meadows, IL 60007
708/555-3839

JOB OBJECTIVE

Public relations director for Hot Fun Sunglasses Co.

ACCOMPLISHMENTS & ACHIEVEMENTS

* Managed a sales/marketing staff which included account managers and sales representatives.
* Represented company to clients and retailers in order to present new products.
* Monitored and studied the effectiveness of a national distribution network.
* Organized and planned convention displays and strategy.
* Designed and executed direct mail campaign that identified marketplace needs and new options for products.
* Oversaw all aspects of sales/marketing budget.
* Conceived ads, posters and point-of-purchase materials for products.
* Initiated and published a monthly newsletter that was distributed to current and potential customers.

WORK HISTORY

Hot Fun Sunglasses Co., Schaumburg, IL

National Sales Manager, 1987 - present
Account Manager, 1985 - 1987
Assistant Account Manager, 1984 -1985
Research Assistant, 1982 - 1984
Secretary, 1980 - 1982

EDUCATION

Indiana University, Bloomington, IN
B.A. in Economics, 1979

SEMINARS

National Marketing Association Seminars, 1985 - 1990

SPECIAL SKILLS

Computer programming experience and database and spreadsheet skills.

References available

MARILYN CICCONE

1 S. Earl Road
Detroit, MI 33290
313/555-3434

OBJECTIVE

A management position in marketing where I can utilize my promotion and public relations experience.

WORK EXPERIENCE

BUBBA BURGER INC., Detroit, MI
Marketing Director, 1986 - present
Developed a successful marketing campaign for a fast food restaurant chain. Initiated and maintained a positive working relationship with radio and print media. Implemented marketing strategies to increase sales at less profitable outlets. Designed a training program for store managers and staff.

CHE COSMETICS CO., Harrisburg, MI
Marketing Representative, 1982 -1986
Demonstrated perfume products in specialty and department stores. Reported customer reactions to manufacturers. Designed fliers and advertising to promote products. Made frequent calls to retail outlets.

CHEWY GUM, INC., Chicago, IL
Assistant to Sales Manager, 1977 - 1982
Handled both internal and external areas of sales and marketing, including samples, advertising and pricing. Served as company sales representative and sold carpeting to retail outlets.

EDUCATION

UCLA, Los Angeles, CA
B.A. Marketing, 1976

SEMINARS

Michigan Marketing Workshop, 1988, 1989
Sales and Marketing Association Seminars, 1984

References available on request.

MARION STEVENSON

2782 W. 57th St.   202/555-8908
Washington, DC 02390   202/555-7200

OBJECTIVE: A position in sales or marketing for an importer
                  of fine products.

WORK
EXPERIENCE: Sandler Imports, Washington, DC
                  Sales Coordinator, 1987 - present
                  Managed ten field representatives. Handled
                  information dissemination and distribution. Co-
                  designed a full-color catalog. Placed advertising
                  in major trade publications. Promoted products at
                  trade shows. Maintained inventory status reports
                  and personnel records.

                  HTQ Publishing Co., Owings Mills, MD
                  Distribution Assistant, 1980 - 1987
                  Developed new distribution outlets through cold-
                  calls and follow-up visits. Increased
                  distribution in my district by 45% over a three-
                  year period. Coordinated a direct mail program
                  that increased magazine subscriptions 120%.

                  Eastman Kodak Co., Atlanta, GA
                  Sales representative, 1975 -1980
                  Sold and serviced office copiers to businesses and
                  schools in the greater Atlanta area. Maintained
                  good customer relations through frequent calls and
                  visits. Identified potential customers.

EDUCATION: Georgetown University, Washington, DC
                  B.S. in Communications, 1974

PROFESSIONAL
MEMBERSHIPS: National Association of Importers
                  DC Community Association
                  Lion's Club

REFERENCES: Available on request.

MOSES WASHINGTON
1783 W. Irving Park Road
Chicago, IL 60625
312/555-4890

OBJECTIVE: A position as a sales representative which involves direct sales and account management.

WORK
EXPERIENCE: <u>Shasta, Inc.</u>, Chicago, IL
Salesman, 1987 - 1990
Sold soft drink products to retail businesses. Named top salesman of 1986. Maintained good customer relations by identifying customer needs. Trained new sales representatives and advised them on effective selling techniques.

<u>Hilgrad Typewriter Co.</u>, Aurora, IL
Salesman, 1982 - 1987
Sold typewriters to offices in the South suburban Chicago area. Increased territory sales by 85% in five years. Demonstrated and planned specific uses for products in various offices. Maintained constant contact with accounts.

EDUCATION: <u>Hilgrad Sales Training Course</u>, Aurora, IL
Summer 1982

<u>Lane Technical High School</u>, Chicago, IL
Graduated 1981
Football Team, Co-captain

REFERENCES: Available upon request

MORRIS DAY
14141 S. Michigan Ave. #342
Chicago, IL 60602

JOB OBJECTIVE

A position as a sales/marketing representative for a manufacturer of lighting equipment.

PROFESSIONAL ACHIEVEMENTS

Sales

*Established and maintained an excellent relationship with over 100 accounts in the lighting equipment industry.
*Resolved customer complaints promptly.
*Provided customers with detailed information on products and replacement parts.
*Named salesperson of the month six times.

Marketing

*Demonstrated the value of quantity purchases to customers.
*Researched industry competition to refine selling techniques.
*Projected success of new products through surveys and questionnaires.

WORK HISTORY

General Electric, Inc., Aurora, IL
Sales Representative, 1987 - present

Republic Electronics, New Orleans, LA
Salesperson, 1984 - 1987

EDUCATION

Southern University, New Orleans, LA
1982 - 1984

Ellis High School, New Orleans, LA
Graduated 1982

REFERENCES

Available upon request

Johanna Farac

152 S. Fedner Drive
Omaha, NE 73802

402/555-9000 (Day)
402/555-6712 (Evening)

JOB OBJECTIVE

A position as a management trainee with a major bookstore retail chain selling to all trade areas.

WORK EXPERIENCE

Crown Books, Inc., Omaha, NE
Assistant Sales Manager, 1989 - present

Sold books, waited on customers, filled mail orders, handled special orders, and took care of returned merchandise. Contributed to window displays. Handled the placing of ads for a major advertising campaign. Represented store at conventions.

Fern Books, Fernwood, NE
Salesperson, 1987 - 1988

Sold books to customers, filled special orders, organized and arranged inventory. Handled customer complaints and special requests.

EDUCATION

Omaha High School, Omaha, NE
Graduated June 1988
Ranked 12 in a class of 320
Worked in student bookstore four years.

REFERENCES

Provided on request

CAROL LINDERMAN
Snadler Hall
144 Glendon Ave.
Room 225
Los Angeles, CA 90289
213/555-2384

EDUCATION

UCLA, Los Angeles, CA
Bachelor of Arts in Economics
Expected June 1991

HONORS

Phi Beta Kappa
Dean's List four semesters
Peter J. Tolbrook Award, 1989

ACTIVITIES

President, Student Government
Freshman Advisor
Homecoming Planning Committee
Volleyball Team

WORK EXPERIENCE

NBC, Inc., Burbank, CA
Sales Intern, 1990
Assisted sales staff in the areas of research,
demographics, sales forecasts, identifying new
customers and promotion.

UCLA, Los Angeles, CA
Research/Office Assistant, 1988-89
Researched and compiled materials for department
professors. Arranged filing system and supervisor's
library. Organized department inventory.

SPECIAL SKILLS

Fluent in Spanish. Experience using WORDSTAR and dBASE
III software programs.

References available on request

YOLANDA RICHARDS

6600 Manhattan Ave.
Brooklyn, NY 10090
718/555-9656

JOB OBJECTIVE:	Vice President of sales and marketing for Focus Lens, Inc.

PROFESSIONAL EXPERIENCE:

<u>Focus Lens, Inc.</u>, New York, NY
Sales Manager, 1984 - present
Sold custom designed point-of-purchase elements and product displays. Researched target areas and developed new account leads. Researched and determined advertising in national publications. Made sales presentations to potential customers. Participated in lens industry trade shows.

<u>Redheart Lawn Co.</u>, Forest Lawn, NY
District Sales Manager, 1981 - 1983
Planned successful sales strategies in order to identify and develop new accounts. Supervised seven sales representatives. Increased sales by at least 20% in each of my four years. Researched and analyzed market conditions to seek out new customers. Wrote monthly sales reports.

<u>Ace Office Supply Co.</u>, Brooklyn, NY
Account Executive, 1978 - 1981
Managed accounts in the New York metropolitan area. Expanded customer base 30% in four years. Maintained daily contact with customers by telephone in order to insure good customer/company relations. Wrote product information fliers and distributed them through a direct mail program.

EDUCATION:

<u>Northwestern University</u>, Evanston, IL
M.B.A. with honors, 1977

<u>Drake University</u>, Des Moines, IA
B.A. in Accounting, 1974

PROFESSIONAL MEMBERSHIPS:

Brooklyn Sales Association, 1983 - present
New York Merchants Group, 1981 - present

REFERENCES: Available upon request

MICHELLE WOODS
1201 W. PORTER AVE.
OAK PARK, IL 60302
708/555-9000
708/555-9492

OBJECTIVE

Vice President of Operations at Osco Drug Co.

WORK EXPERIENCE

Osco Drug Co., Oak Park, IL
Manager of Operations, 1982 - present

Supervised marketing, production, distribution and accounting.
Introduced and developed a computer system in order to provide
accurate inventory controls. Achieved efficiency savings of over
$100,000.00 during system's first year of operation.

Osco Drug Co, Oak Park, IL
Product Manager, 1980 - 1982

Initiated several new products that resulted in high profit margins
for the company. Coordinated research, production, and promotional
programs. Introduced new packaging concepts.

Osco Drug Co., Oak Park, IL
Regional Sales Manager, 1978 - 1980

Supervised 34 brokers and salespeople. Increased sales 40% through
through special marketing programs. Developed better customer
distribution at lower costs.

Osco Drug Co., Oak Park, IL
District Manager, 1977 - 1978

Handled sales in Chicago area. Increased profits 19% in my first
year. Promoted to Regional Manager after one year.

Jewel Food Stores, Inc., Melrose Park, IL
Sales Representative, 1974 - 1977

Sold to wholesalers and chain stores in the midwest. Opened many
new accounts that previous sales representatives could not open.

OTHER ACHIEVEMENTS

Marketing consultant for private businesses.
Wrote a book on product efficiency.
Contributor to various trade journals.

Michelle Woods - 2

EDUCATION

<u>University of Michigan</u>, Ann Arbor, MI
B.S., 1972
Major in Business, minor in Economics

Attended seminars at Simmons Institute, Cleveland, OH and
J.L. Kellogg School of Management, Evanston, IL

PROFESSIONAL MEMBERSHIPS

National Management Association
Lion's Club, Board of Directors
Midwest Sales Affiliates

REFERENCES

Available upon request

LEONARD PHILLIP SCHROEDER

1550 W. HARBOR DRIVE
CHICAGO, IL 60614
312/555-1434 (DAY)
312/555-3333 (NIGHT)

JOB OBJECTIVE

Marketing manager for a company that manufactures auto parts.

PROFESSIONAL EXPERIENCE

Marketing

* Researched competitive products in order to evaluate
competitors' strengths and weaknesses.
* Planned a marketing strategy that resulted in a
significant increase in accounts.
* Maintained demographic data in order to ascertain buyer
profile.

Sales and Promotion

* Made cold calls and visits to sporting goods retailers
which resulted in increased accounts.
* Visited and serviced existing accounts to encourage
continued sales.
* Advised customers on options available to meet a wide
range of product needs.
* Handled dealer requests for information and sample
products.

EMPLOYMENT HISTORY

Sears Automotive, Inc., Chicago, IL
Assistant Sales Manager, 1985 - present
Sales Representative, 1983 - 1985

Teychert Co., Chicago, IL
Marketing Assistant, 1982

Royal Crown Cola, Inc., Cicero, IL
Salesperson, 1980 - 1982

Baker's Square Restaurant, Lincolnwood, IL
Waiter, 1979 - 1980

LEONARD PHILLIP SCHROEDER - 2

EDUCATION

<u>Eastern Illinois University</u>, Carbondale, IL
B.A. in Marketing, 1982

HONORS

Phi Beta Kappa, 1982
Dean's List, 1980 - 1982
Harrison Marketing Scholarship Recipient, 1980, 1981
President, Student Activities Board, 1982

SPECIAL SKILLS

Experience using a variety of word processing, data base and spreadsheet software. Knowledge of German and French.

REFERENCES

Provided on request

Chapter Six

SAMPLE COVER LETTERS

KENNETH THOMAS PARKER
1400 N. LAKE SHORE DRIVE
CHICAGO, IL 60601

September 2, 1990

Ms. Sandra Watt
Human Resources
Porter Sporting Goods, Inc.
133 W. York Ave.
Schiller Park, IL 60027

Dear Ms. Watt:

I am inquiring into the possibility of an opening for a Sales Manager
at Porter. I am enclosing my resume for your consideration if such an
opening occurs in the near future.

Currently, I am employed as Assistant Sales Manager for Wilson Sporting
Goods where I have been employed since 1985. My experience in sporting
goods sales includes cold calls and visits to retailers which resulted in
increased accounts, research of competitive products to evaluate strengths
and weaknesses of competitors and the planning of successful marketing
strategies.

I am interested in parlaying my experience into a management level
position. I have always admired Porter's foresight and innovation and
would like to be a part of Porter's future.

Please let me know if you are hiring at the present time as I would be
interested in interviewing with you. Thank you for your consideration.

Sincerely,

Kenneth Thomas Parker

MOSES WASHINGTON
1723 W. Irving Park Road
Chicago, IL 60625

July 29, 1990

Joe Perlman
Sales Manager
Shasta, Inc.
45 E. Huron St.
Chicago, IL 60623

Dear Mr. Perlman:

I noticed your posting regarding an opening for Sales Coordinator here
at Shasta. I would like to formally apply for this position.

As you know, I have been working here at Shasta for the last three and
a half years as a salesman. My responsibilities have included selling
soft drink products to retail, indentifying customer needs and training
new salespeople. I feel that I am ready for a promotion and that I
am qualified for this position.

I would like to interview with you at your convenience. Please call me
at ext. #422 or at home at 312/555-8928. I look forward to hearing from
you soon regarding this opportunity.

Sincerely,

Moses Washington

DONALD E. THOMPSON
1314 W. Dundee Road
Buffalo Grove, IL 60006

March 30, 1990

Mr. Henry Corleone
Branch Manager Sales
Datatech Computer Co.
4444 E. Monroe
Chicago, IL 60606

Dear Mr. Corleone:

Please consider me for the position of Assistant Branch Manager of Sales
at Datatech. I am enclosing my resume for your perusal. I learned of
this opening through Computer Weekly and through a colleague of mine
at Microtech.

My experience in the computer industry dates back thirty years and
encompasses several different areas. Most recently, I have served as
Account Executive for Microtech where I handle sales accounts for the
northwest suburban area. Before that, I worked for IBM in the capacity of
Technical Support Specialist and Systems Analyst.

I believe that I could bring my expertise in these diverse areas to Datatech
and thus enhance your present, quite talented sales division.

I will be calling next week to follow up this letter and to inquire as to
the possibility of an interview.

Sincerely,

Donald E. Thompson
708/555-3909

LISA STANSFIELD
14 E. ThreePenny Road
Detroit, MI 33290
313/555-3489

4/18/90

Zan Marketing
500 E. Hubbard St.
Detroit, MI 33909
Attn: Hilda C. Roane

Dear Ms. Roane:

I am interested in applying for your opening for a Marketing Manager
at Zan Marketing. I learned of this opening from your ad in the
Detroit Free Press.

Currently, I am employed as Marketing Director for Seven Eleven, Inc.
here in Detroit. Some of my accomplishments at this company include
the development of a successful marketing campaign, the implementation
of marketing strategies to increase sales at less profitable outlets
and the designing of a training program for store managers and staff.

Zan's positive reputation is well-known throughout the industry and
I am most interested in helping to perpetuate that reputation.

Please feel free to call me for an interview. My resume is enclosed.

Best Regards,

Lisa Stansfield

February 27, 1990

Hollywood Reporter
Box 1140-H
465 Hollywood Way
Burbank, CA 91505

To Whom It May Concern:

I am responding to your ad in <u>The Hollywood Reporter</u> that ran on 2/14/90 for a marketing assistant at a major Hollywood production company. I am enclosing my resume and salary requirements as requested.

I am a recent graduate of California State University at Northridge where I received a B.A. in Business. My work experience includes an internship at Warner Bros. Studios in Burbank in the market research department. My goal is to work in the marketing department of an entertainment corporation.

I am anxious to learn more about this position and look forward to hearing from you soon. Please feel free to call me at home or at work. Thank you for your time and consideration.

Sincerely,

Ken Phillips
3323 Effingham Place
Los Angeles, CA 90027

213/555-7648 (Home)
213/555-3333 (Work)

August 23, 1990

David Bascombe III
Sears & Roebuck, Inc.
1000 S. Adams
Chicago, IL 60601

Dear Mr. Bascombe:

I am responding to your job listing for a Marketing Management Trainee which was posted in the placement office at Boston University. I am interested in applying for this position and therefore I am enclosing my resume with this letter.

I have recently graduated from Boston University with a degree in Economics and I am anxious to find a position the marketing field. I also plan on working towards a Master's in Marketing in the future, probably by taking evening courses.

My work experience includes employment as a Marketing Assistant for Lewis Advertising Agency in Boston and as a Telephone Surveyor for Paterno Marketing.

I will be in the Chicago area the week of 9/12. Would it be possible to set up an interview with you during that week? If so, please contact me at your earliest convenience.

Sincerly,

Janis Darien
345 W. 3rd St.
#42
Boston, MA 02210
617/555-3291

```
              JEREMY S. PANDY
              1441 S. GOEBERT
           PROVIDENCE, RI   00231
```

March 11, 1990

Anderson Publishing Inc.
1000 7th Avenue
Suite 1000
New York, NY 10019
Attn: Delores Darnell
       Director of Personnel

Dear Ms. Darnell:

Through your recent press release, I became aware of the recent departure of your company's president, Myron Strickland. With that in mind, I am forwarding my resume to you for your consideration in your search for a new president.

With over twenty years of experience in the publishing industry, including most currently Vice President of Advertising at Johnson Publishing in Providence, I feel that I have the experience and the industry knowledge to tackle this challenge. My employment history also includes stints with Rebus Publishing and Time Magazine.

I believe that Anderson Publishing is a company with a future and I am convinced that I can help shape that future. I expect great things from myself and Anderson.

I will be following up this letter with a telephone call next week. I will be in New York City during the week of 3/20 and would be happy to meet with you regarding this position at that time.

Thank you for your kind consideration.

Sincerely,

Jeremy S. Pandy
401/555-1234
401/555-3782

May 15, 1990

Deborah Klugh
Director of Human Resources
NBC
1220 Rockefeller Plaza
New York, NY 10019

Dear Ms. Klugh:

This letter is in repsonse to your ad in <u>The New York Times</u> for a sales
assistant. Enclosed are my resume and salary requirements as requested
in your ad.

Next month I will be graduating from Boston University with degree in
Business Administration and a concentration in Sales Management. I was
inducted into Phi Beta Kappa this month and expect to graduate with honors
in June.

I am interested in working in the television industry in a sales capacity and
would be most pleased to be a part of the NBC team.

Please contact me if you are interested. I am willing to travel to New York
for an interview if necessary. Thank you for your time and consideration.

Sincerely,

Barton T. Quigley
Boston University
Fenton Hall
199 W. Hampshire Way
Boston, MA 02201
602/555-3839

SALLY JOHANSON

3240 Santa Monica Blvd.
Los Angeles, CA 90028

December 20, 1990

David G. Sandler
Director of Human Resources
Nessex Motor Co.
12000 Wilshire Blvd.
Santa Monica, CA 90390

Dear Mr. Sandler:

I am interested in applying for the position of Assistant Manager at
your Nessex dealership in Santa Monica. Your ad in The L.A. Times
alerted me to this opening.

I am currently a sales representative for Yugo in Los Angeles where
I have handled, besides sales, market analyses, research, forecasts
and service and billing problems.

I have held this position for three years and am now ready to explore
new challenges in auto sales--assistant manager being one on them. I
feel I am qualified for this job.

Enclosed is my resume. Please take me into consideration. I look
forward to interviewing with you.

Sincerely,

Sally Johanson
213/555-9832 (Home)
213/555-2121 (Work)

JAMES KENDALL
509 27th St., #4556
New York, NY 10019

July 29, 1990

Peterson & Co.
111 W. Monroe St.
Chicago, IL 60660
Attn: David L. Snowheart

Dear Mr. Snowheart:

I am interested in applying for a Commodity Broker position at your
company. I heard through a fellow broker at Jones and Jones that you
were currently hiring, and therefore I am forwarding my resume to you.

I have been in the commodities business for the past fifteen years.
During that time, I gained experience as a trader, a sales representative
and finally as a broker for Jones and Jones in New York. I currently
handle over 500 clients as a specialist in corn and wheat futures. I also
publish and distribute a weekly newsletter on futures.

In the late 70s, in worked for Pickering, Pickering & Gold in Chicago and
I hope to return to Chicago to work for your company in the near future.
Please feel free to contact me for an interview at 212/555-9809 (Day) or
212/555-7777 (Evening).

                    Sincerely,

                    James Kendall

January 30, 1990

Robert T. Beatty
Director of Personnel
Turner Broadcasting Co.
One Turner Plaza
Atlanta, GA 33203

Dear Mr. Beatty:

I am writing to you regarding the possibilty of obtaining a position
within your company in the area of advertising sales.

I have several years of sales experience behind me, including work for
Medialink Advertising Agency in San Francisco and KTUT-TV in Portland.
As you can see from my resume, I have sold space for major clients in
the automotive industry, advised on the content and suitability of ads,
and have done demographic research.

My desire at this time is to break into cable television because I believe
it has a bright future and I want to be a part of that future. Please
review my resume and advise as to the feasibility of an interview.

Sincerely,

Sandra T. Pearson
12 E. Tenth St.
San Francisco, CA 94890
415/555-2343

JOHN L. RYDER
211 W. FOURTH ST. #211
BROOKLYN, NY 10001
718/555-9080

June 12, 1990

John Junot
Fidelity Insurance Co.
1440 W. 57th St.
New York, NY 10019

Dear Mr. Junot:

I am responding to your advertisement for a Sales Manager/East Coast for your insurance company. As you asked, I am enclosing my resume and a list of references.

After several years working as an agent and an adjustor, I feel that I am ready to make the move into a management position and I believe that a position of this kind at Fidelity would benefit both me and the company. My vast experience in the insurance industry has prepared me well for this next step in my career.

Please review my resume and let me know if and when you would like me to come to your office for an interview. I look forward to meeting with you.

Sincerely,

John L. Ryder

JOHANNA FARAC
152 S. Fedner Drive
Omaha, NE 73802

September 30, 1990

Susan P. Evers
Federated Books, Inc.
1442 S. 7th Ave.
Omaha, NE 73092

Dear Ms. Evers:

I am responding to your ad in The Omaha Register for a management trainee
for your book store. Enclosed is my resume and salary requirements as
you requested.

All of my life I have had a fascination for books and bookstores. In
high school I worked in the student bookstores all four years and my
work experience includes stints as a salesperson for Fern Books and
as assistant sales manager for Crown Books in Omaha.

Thank you for your time and consideration. I look forward to hearing
from you and meeting with you soon.

Sincerely,

Johanna Farac
402/555-9000 (Day)
402/555-6712 (Evening)

DAVID P. JENKINS
3663 N. COLDWATER CANYON
NORTH HOLLYWOOD, CA   90390
818/555-3472
818/555-3678

July 29, 1990

Mr. Jeremy Hitleman
Vice President of Sales and Marketing
Sandoval Industries
500 University Drive
Santa Barbara, CA   97809

Dear Mr. Hitleman:

I am writing to you to inquire about the possibility of obtaining a
position with Sandoval Industries as a sales/marketing manager.

My special interest in working for your company stems from a desire
to expand my experience into the area of hardware sales. Your company's
recent addition of a hardware division brought Sandoval to my attention.

Currently, I serve as regional sales manager for Tribor Industries where
I represent five corporate divisions with sales in excess of $3,000,000
annually. Previous to this position, I served as district manager for
Tribor.

I believe that my sales experience well qualifies me for a position
at Sandoval Industries. Please call me for an interview if you feel the
same. Enclosed is my resume.

Sincerely,

David P. Jenkins

JERRY MATHEWS, JR.
6701 N. Mariposa Ave.
Boise, ID 83209
919/555-3402

October 2, 1990

Paul H. Harrison
Vice President of Marketing
Boise Electric Corporation
4000 N. Agricultural Blvd.
Boise, ID 84203

Dear Mr. Harrision:

The purpose of this letter is to inquire into the possibility
of full-time employment as a sales representative for Boise Electric
Corporation.

As my enclosed resume indicates, I have seven years of experience in
sales with three different companies. Currently, I am a sales assistant
for Codaphone, Inc., a company which sells telephone equipment to
businesses. I both sell and service accounts.

I am looking for a job that is more challenging that the one I
presently have and I feel that Boise Electric is the company that
can offer me that challenge.

Is it possible for us to meet and discuss my qualifications and goals?
If so, please contact me as soon as possible for an interview.

Best regards,

Jerry Mathews, Jr.

August 12, 1990

Felicia Robertson
Gandy's Fine Jewelry
2300 S. Vermont Ave.
Los Angeles, CA 90380

Dear Ms. Robertson:

I am enclosing my resume for consideration for any sales opening you may currently have. James Gooden, who works at your store, gave me your name and told me you may have a opening soon.

I have always wanted to work for Gandy's. I believe it to be the best fine jewelry store in southern California. My past experience includes sales work at Stacey's Jewelers in Chatsworth and Eddy Gems in Glendale. My skills include greeting customers and advising them on their needs and designing window displays.

I would be more than willing to come in for an interview if you feel that I am qualified for the position. Thank you for considering me.

Sincerely,

Melanie B. Maloney
1200 Puerta Del Sol
Chatsworth, CA 92203
714/555-6789

WINONA T. SIMPSON
420 W. Easterly Avenue
Indianapolis, IN   49091

September 2, 1990

Thomas E. Eagletender
Pizza Hut, Inc.
4200 Bolt Ave.
Indianapolis, IN   48902

Dear Mr. Eagletender:

David Porter of your marketing department informed me that you were
looking for a new P.R. manager for your midwest office. Therefore,
I am sending along my resume for your consideration in regards to this
position.

Currently, I serve as P.R. Director for Blockbuster Video in Indianapolis
where I have been since 1985. Before that I worked as marketing
representative for Jeron Stereo and as P.R. assistant for Kader
Advertising.

My accomplishments include developing a successful marketing campaign for
Blockbuster, implementing marketing strategies to increase sales at less
profitable outlets and designing a training program for store managers
and staff.

I believe my resume speaks for itself. I would very much like to meet
with you to discuss this position further. Please contact me at
317/555-1212 at your convenience.

Sincerely,

Winona T. Simpson

August 23, 1990

Steven R. Stevens
Red Man Furnace Co.
7892 Collins Ave.
Miami, FL 08902

Dear Mr. Stevens:

I am responding to your advertisement for a Sales Manager in the Miami Herald
of August 18, 1990. I am interested in such a position and as a result I am
forwarding my resume to you.

My sales experience is extensive and goes back ten years. As an account
executive for Newmark Furnace Co., I have handled sales accounts in the
south Florida area and expanded my customer base by 28% in the last three
years. Previous to that, I worked as a sales representative for Potisco
in Terre Haute, IN and Honoco in Chicago, IL.

I feel I am qualified for the position you are currently interviewing for.
If, after reviewing my resume, you feel the same, please contact me for
an interview. Thank you.

Sincerely,

Patrick H. McCoy
1701 N. Hampshire Pl.
Miami, FL 03908
305/555-3909
305/555-9099

GINA CAROL STONE
5001 Lincoln Drive #2
Marlton, NJ 08053
609/555-1200
609/555-3893

August 23, 1990

Howard G. Flagellum
Director of Personnel
Best Paper Products, Inc.
500 E. 3rd St.
Suite 1100
Trenton, NJ 08390

Dear Mr. Flagellum:

I am interested in being considered for any openings you may have at
the present time in sales management. Enclosed please find my resume.

As District Sales Manager for Harrison Paper Co. in Philadelphia, I have
developed valuable skills that well qualify me for a management position
in your company. After seven years at Harrison, I am ready for a change,
but I want to continue to work within the paper products industry.

Some of my accomplishments at Harrison include increased sales each year,
supervision of seven sales representatives and extensive market research
which led to the establishment of several new accounts.

I would be free to interview   at any time. Please let me know if
you are currently hiring in this area. Thank you for your time and
consideration.

                    Sincerely,

                    Gina Carol Stone

CAROL A BADEN
150 FORT WASHINGTON AVE.
NEW YORK, NY 10032
212/555-2498

May 14, 1990

Dana Jacobs
Human Resources
AT&T
1000 E. 5th Ave.
New York, NY 10090

Dear Ms. Jacobs:

David Sanderson, who works in the marketing department at AT&T, suggested that I contact you regarding a possible management trainee position in your sales department. I am enclosing my resume for your consideration.

I will be graduating this month from New York University with a degree in Communications. I was recently inducted into the Communications Honor Society (Beta Alpha Psi) and I am a member of the Association for International Business (A.I.S.E.C.).

I am interested in working in the communications industry in a sales division and I feel the best place for me to start would be as a management trainee at AT&T.

I will be calling you in about a week to follow up on this letter. Please feel free to call Mr. Sanderson for a reference.

Sincerely,

Carol A. Baden

VGM CAREER BOOKS

OPPORTUNITIES IN
Available in both paperback and hardbound editions

Accounting Careers
Acting Careers
Advertising Careers
Aerospace Careers
Agriculture Careers
Airline Careers
Animal and Pet Care
Appraising Valuation Science
Architecture
Automotive Service
Banking
Beauty Culture
Biological Sciences
Biotechnology Careers
Book Publishing Careers
Broadcasting Careers
Building Construction Trades
Business Communication Careers
Business Management
Cable Television
Carpentry Careers
Chemical Engineering
Chemistry Careers
Child Care Careers
Chiropractic Health Care
Civil Engineering Careers
Commercial Art and Graphic Design
Computer Aided Design and
    Computer Aided Mfg.
Computer Maintenance Careers
Computer Science Careers
Counseling & Development
Crafts Careers
Culinary Careers
Dance
Data Processing Careers
Dental Care
Drafting Careers
Electrical Trades
Electronic and Electrical Engineering
Electronics Careers
Energy Careers
Engineering Careers
Engineering Technology Careers
Environmental Careers
Eye Care Careers
Fashion Careers
Fast Food Careers
Federal Government Careers
Film Careers
Financial Careers
Fire Protection Services
Fitness Careers
Food Services
Foreign Language Careers
Forestry Careers
Gerontology Careers
Government Service
Graphic Communications
Health and Medical Careers
High Tech Careers
Home Economics Careers
Hospital Administration
Hotel & Motel Management
Human Resources Management
    Careers
Information Systems Careers

Insurance Careers
Interior Design
International Business
Journalism Careers
Landscape Architecture
Laser Technology
Law Careers
Law Enforcement and Criminal Justice
Library and Information Science
Machine Trades
Magazine Publishing Careers
Management
Marine & Maritime Careers
Marketing Careers
Materials Science
Mechanical Engineering
Medical Technology Careers
Metalworking Careers
Microelectronics
Military Careers
Modeling Careers
Music Careers
Newspaper Publishing Careers
Nursing Careers
Nutrition Careers
Occupational Therapy Careers
Office Occupations
Opticianry
Optometry
Packaging Science
Paralegal Careers
Paramedical Careers
Part-time & Summer Jobs
Performing Arts Careers
Petroleum Careers
Pharmacy Careers
Photography
Physical Therapy Careers
Physician Careers
Plastics Careers
Plumbing & Pipe Fitting
Podiatric Medicine
Printing Careers
Property Management Careers
Psychiatry
Psychology
Public Health Careers
Public Relations Careers
Purchasing Careers
Real Estate
Recreation and Leisure
Refrigeration and Air Conditioning
Religious Service
Restaurant Careers
Retailing
Robotics Careers
Sales Careers
Sales & Marketing
Secretarial Careers
Securities Industry
Social Science Careers
Social Work Careers
Speech-Language Pathology Careers
Sports & Athletics
Sports Medicine
State and Local Government
Teaching Careers
Technical Communications
Telecommunications
Television and Video Careers

Theatrical Design & Production
Transportation Careers
Travel Careers
Trucking Careers
Veterinary Medicine Careers
Vocational and Technical Careers
Welding Careers
Word Processing
Writing Careers
Your Own Service Business

CAREERS IN
Accounting; Advertising; Business; Communications; Computers; Education; Engineering; Health Care; Law; Marketing; Science

CAREER DIRECTORIES
Careers Encyclopedia
Occupational Outlook Handbook

CAREER PLANNING
Admissions Guide to Selective
    Business Schools
Career Planning and Development for
    College Students and Recent
    Graduates
Careers Checklists
Careers for Animal Lovers
Careers for Bookworms
Careers for Foreign Language
    Aficionados
Careers for Good Samaritans
Careers for Sport Nuts
Careers for Travel Buffs
Guide to Basic Resume Writing
Handbook of Business and
    Management Careers
Handbook of Scientific and
    Technical Careers
How to Change Your Career
How to Choose the Right Career
How to Get and Get Ahead
    On Your First Job
How to Get People to Do Things
    Your Way
How to Have a Winning Job Interview
How to Land a Better Job
How to Make the Right Career Moves
How to Prepare for College
How to Run Your Own Home Business
How to Succeed in High School
How to Write a Winning Resume
Joyce Lain Kennedy's Career Book
Life Plan
Planning Your Career of Tomorrow
Planning Your College Education
Planning Your Military Career
Planning Your Young Child's
    Education
Resumes for Communications Careers
Resumes for High Tech Careers
Resumes for Sales and Marketing Careers

SURVIVAL GUIDES
Dropping Out or Hanging In
High School Survival Guide
College Survival Guide

VGM Career Horizons
a division of *NTC Publishing Group*
4255 West Touhy Avenue
Lincolnwood, Illinois 60646-1975